Is your Business Ready?

For the Social Media Revolution

Peter B. Giblett

P3 Social Media

Toronto ♦ New York

Is your Business Ready? For the Social Media Revolution

By Peter B. Giblett

FIRST EDITION

Originally published by P3 Social Media in 2010.

Currently this work is not registered with either the British Library Integrated Catalogue or with the Library of Congress Catalog.

EAN/ISBN-13: 9781452846804

ISBN: 1452846804

P3 Social Media is available at +1 905 371 3908 or +1 646 875 4558

9 8 7 6 5 4 3 2 1 0

I would like to thank three people for making this book happen. ***Firstly***, *Peter Widdis, for his patience and listening to my ramblings over the past few months, and subsequent encouragement.* ***Secondly***, *Paul Lalley, for suggesting that I once again consider again self-publishing, rather than seeking a more traditional publisher.* ***Thirdly,*** *and most importantly my loving wife Afroz for being there and supporting me in the ways she knows best.*

Contents

Foreword By Peter Widdis

Are You Ready? Let's just say I was one of those business people who were not. Candidly speaking, I used to be somewhat anti-social (when it came to the cyber world that is). I was probably the furthest thing from being a tech savvy person of any sort, often having the IT department on speed dial from my office desk. Recognizing the online world moved in waves, with the majority of businesses following a trend not because it was fashionable but out of commercial necessity, I continued to stay on the periphery, somewhat skeptical of being more social with any cyber space marketing endeavors. After all, first our brands had to go online, just to be online, then, there was the importance of ad words, followed by blogging and podcasts. So what really made Social Media any different?

Upon researching this so called new holy grail of internet communication, I came to the initial conclusion that Social Media was yet another catchall specialty marketing phrase, invented by some clever on-line entrepreneur, encompassing any website that offered interactive functionality and user-generated content capabilities. From social networks to video sharing to social news hubs, I was convinced the strategic impetus behind Social Media was once again to build awareness, drive sales, elicit endless buzz, save the world, etc. etc. That was until I met Peter Giblett.

Peter showed me that Social Media is so much (much) more. That Social Media is as much a conversational art forum for human beings as it is a collaborative forum for game-changing breakthroughs in both the private and public sectors. He opened my eyes to the innovation enabler Social Media truly is and both the accessibility and opportunity it afforded anyone who dreamt of a more emotively connected global community. He taught me that Social Media was not just new media terminology. Fundamentally, through Peter Giblett's coaching seminars, I quickly realized Social Media is rapidly becoming a way of life that is not going away anytime soon!

Overall, any businessperson in the world today, seeking Social Media guidance, will be inspired by *"Is Your Business Ready for the Social Media Revolution?"* Whether working in a start-up or operating in a mature industry, anyone who aspires to fulfill their career passions or simply move the sales needle, needs to absorb Peter Giblet's Social Media teachings embedded within the pages of this dynamic read. When it comes to making it as easy as possible for people to collaborate, connect their knowledge and skills with others using Social Media, everyone can learn a lot from Peter Giblett. Through his understanding of the motivations and technical mechanisms for online customer engagement, he will open your mind to Social Media possibilities that truly quantify ROI.

Peter's *"Is Your Business Ready for the Social Media Revolution?"* has not only converted me into an evangelist of the connectivity inherent to the medium - I now believe in the power of socializing as much as advertising.

Thanks! I can hardly wait for the sequel.

Peter Widdis

Senior Consultant, Stratovation™ Associates, Inc.

Professor, George Brown College

Foreword About the Author

Peter B. Giblett is a Senior Consulting, Marketing and IT Executive who has more than 25 years experience delivering successful solutions. He spent most of his working life in Europe, but has also delivered solutions to top corporations across the world.

He was born in the London England, but now resides in resides in rural Ontario and is currently working with clients in Canada and the USA in order to develop their Social Media policies. His interest is Social Media corporate restructuring at a time when this new media was coming to public attention. He has taken the time to research this new developing world over the past three years.

His research into social media has brought him into contact with dozens of senior executives and hundreds of their clients, or prospects discussing the whole process of marketing through the internet. In looking at how people use the Internet and specifically the use of social media sites like Twitter, Facebook, and LinkedIn it became clear the there is a transformation in progress in the world on on-line marketing. One aspect that is important to purchasers is trust.

His initial discovery was that many of Internet only corporations have a poor customer services reputation. The only ones that performed well were those that associated their sales process with a scoring system. Combined with this the advent of social media gives customers an ability to communicate with others about the quality of the service provision. To Peter this was the on-line equivalent of his mother talking to her friends about the poor quality of service available from local stores, with the strong recommendation that they stop shopping there. He realised that there social media had an immediate comparison to this earlier era.

This is a very important aspect of marketing through the Internet, without it the prospects for marketing were in decline. He discovered that there were a large number of traditional advertising agencies that sought to diversify their business and leverage the social media channels for the benefit of their clients. Making the jump they were failing to understand the core principles of this media. This is the essence of Peter's book and the work he continues with clients on a daily basis.

Peter is also working with a new Social Media start-up and their President and Chief Innovation Officer. He also publishes a regular column at http://cio-perspectives.com/, and is an active member of Toastmasters.

Introduction

The purpose of this book is to provide a new understanding of how to adapt your business to leverage the new social media channels. Social media is more about personality, how we communicate, and building trust-based relationships than traditional advertising theatre. It is a new way of connecting people and it is starting to impact everyone on this planet.

In building a new book on Social Media it was important not to repeat the tired old advertising formulas. Too many people have already done that, simply moving old media methods to the new world – failing to understand the quintessential difference that this new media brings.

Seeking Success - Do not Expect 'An Overnight Sensation'

According to Lawrence Perry "Social media communication takes time. If you want to experience success in it you must treat it as a full-time endeavour and commit time and effort to it". There are three key elements necessary for successful businesses to leverage the social media channels: building communications and collaborative capabilities; intelligent intervention in the marketplace; generate revenue as a trusted advisor that are core to this book.

"No one has ever experienced overnight success in social media marketing" says Perry and here are some of the reasons why:

- Too many Guru's, Evangelists exists, many coming from traditional PR or Advertising background and most have used Facebook a couple of times.
- They have no consistent approach to present.
- Their advertising agency has recently added social media as a new service without understanding how it functions.
- An expert's network shows that they are not widely connected or active in the Social Media space. Their LinkedIn account has not been updated for years.
- When you Google them by name, it is difficult to find them.
- They don't have an active blog with weekly posts.
- They operate a pay-per-post payment structure.

A special thank-you to Peter Shankman for contributing some of these.

This author's background is in Corporate IT. He has been delivering solutions focused towards both Finance and Marketing elements of corporations for over 20 years. He was also responsible for business development for a small Management Consulting firm, he will never claim to be a marketing expert, despite the protestations of his business partner (a brand specialist) who always insists otherwise.

This book has come about as a result of a study made of social media and how it is understood by corporations, advertising agencies, marketing specialists, IT, and corporate executives. Ultimately there is a recognition that new channels and new opportunities are opening up as more people become active on social networks, some of which are now worldwide phenomena. The world has changed and business has to adapt.

Clearly social media differs greatly from traditional PR and advertising. The traditional mode for advertising is about one-way communication, yet to leverage social media it is essential to build a trust based marketing approach. Yes, Twitter can be a cheap way to advertise, but if advertising is all you are there for then people will soon ignore you, stop following you, or worse block you ensuring they never see what you have to say ever again. It is more appropriate to offer articles that are of value to your listener through the corporate blog and even to point at important industry news.

It is entirely possible to use Social Media for "direct marketing" in order to advertise on Social Media sites like Facebook and MySpace in the traditional mode but that fails to leverage their real power. To focus more accurately on a target demographic can be worthwhile for advertising. BUT there is more to be gained from intervening in the media than advertising on it.

Dell learnt this lesson and got involved with social media early. They provide a broad expertise (about personal computers and Windows), but they also consider that as a direct customer facing organisation they must build relationships with their target audience. They are involved in the media, build trust, and ultimately sales by their approach. On the other-hand looking at CNN's intervention on Twitter. It has over 150,000 followers yet follows less than two-dozen people. They leverage the media for push messages associated with traditional news. On a few occasions recently CNN have been 'late to the party' when publishing the news. On one occasion the BBC in London published a story about an event in the USA four hours before CNN first mentioned it. CNN is clearly guilty of not listening to the twitter stream – they use it to publish news items only. Listening would have fed them news stories as they were happening by the people involved. It would have been possible to have been the first news agency responding instead of the last.

One curious aspect about Twitter is that the majority major news story in the last 12 months have broken on Twitter before being published on any of the traditional media channels. In fact TV news reporters have pointed to pre-existing blogs to get the blow, by blow story of what happened – including expressive photographs of events.

So how does this help business? Where a corporation is engaged in the social media space they are seen as responsive to customer needs.

Arguably this lengthens the sales cycle, particularly in the B2B arena, it also involves offering valuable advice for free and demonstrates expertise to a wider audience. With social media proving expertise in a public forum ultimately wins more sales.

One thing that is certain; social media is not simply about getting involved with Twitter and Facebook, and contributing articles from you own blog. That is simply the starting point. It is important to include this media in your corporate strategy. Also there should be a massive intersection between social media and the ability to measure the results, through Business Intelligence that must be explored in order to generate business results. These elements must be done, but you must also have the tools to perform Social Media Intelligence.

> *Example:*
>
> *An IT service company recently secured a lucrative maintenance contract by being active on Twitter. Their presence and answering questions relevant to a prospect's business secured them a maintenance contract. Being active on the channel and providing expertise for free demonstrates a focus on the customer. Being the expert in the social media space went a long way to generating a trust previous service companies lacked.*

Communicating Effectively, and those 140 Characters

Our ability to communicate is one of the key aspects of our humanity. Sadly communicating effectively is something that few of us do consistently well. It is especially vital to communicate well if you are delivering a message in a small space. This is the essence of most social media communities. The message we deliver causes people to listen to us, or conversely stop listening; so it must be right.

Sites like Twitter, LinkedIn, Plaxo and others all use 140 characters for updates. The keys to communicating effectively in a small amount of space are:

- The message
- Linking to a web page
- Making it meaningful.

THE AMERICAN ISSUE

U.S. IS VOTED DRY

36th STATE RATIFIES DRY AMENDMENT JAN. 16

JANUARY 16, 1919, MOMENTOUS DAY IN WORLD'S HISTORY

The message is the starting point. Social media is a very public form of communication. So what message can you deliver in 140 characters? Surely that is too short to create something really meaningful? Yet millions of messages are delivered this way today. We are so used to it that we even forget they exist. Think of a newspaper headline that grabs the readers attention in order to drive them towards a story underneath.

It is essential to create a reason for people to listen to the remainder of your story. This should be focused and effective. How and what you say are important. It should make people want to know more. Social Media in some respects is about 'spreading the news'. It is personal in so far it is your message – but of course the whole world can find your message if they are mindful to.

Some tips:

- Be involved in conversations – give your opinion;
- spread the word about good things other people do;
- be interesting;
- don't spam people.

> *The reason for the 140 characters is linked with the history of computer communications. It corresponds to the 160 characters for the SMS or text message, except a little chunk is used for data management. This is two lines of 80 character text – the limit of plain text on an old computer terminal from the 1960's or 70's, also used on the original Instant Messaging applications.*

Web Links are necessary because they drive people to the real story, whether it was written by you or someone else. Where exactly do you need to drive people? It is no use telling people about a new story on Christmas sausages then pointing them to the website containing the story (as well as a dozen other items). As well as being next to useless, people will soon tune out. They MUST be pointed directly to the important story – like directing the reader to the right page in a book – you have the bookmark – put a sticky marker on it!

One problem with web addresses is that they can be very long, in some instances they are more than 140 characters in length on their own. This is where a URL shortening service comes in handy. One of the first of these was http://tinyurl.com/ yet there are others like http://is.gd/ (is good) and http://bit.ly/ produce even smaller length links. This allows you to publicise your piece without the link using too many characters.

Making it meaningful is largely a matter of personality. How things are said and what you say are important, yet the sender's personality also adds meaning to the message. Any message also needs to be meaningful to your READERS, or followers more than to the person sending the message. But that is the essence of communication isn't it? Remember though as Confucius once said it is not possible to please everyone all of the time and we should not try to do so. Make your statement, and move on.

It is quite possible to deliver an effective and meaningful message in the 140 character format used by many Social Media sites. To get the best out of the service we also need to give people somewhere else to go – the website with useful information on it.

Why Read this Book?

This book is about ensuring that your business is ready to face the challenges of trading in the Social Media community. The rules are changing – business has always been about relationships, but with Social Media any business can be closer to their customer than they have been for a long time.

In building relationships it is as if we have turned back the clock more than a hundred years – people want to build a trusting relationship the way it was once possible with the local shopkeeper, you knew them and valued their expertise, but every time you shopped at the store they would improve their understanding of you the customer and the choices you made. The relationship was important and very personal. The difference being that today we are looking for these same qualities, yet via a very public forum.

The public forum is key, as the onlooker (or perhaps voyeur) can see everything that is happening and it can also influence their buying patterns. It is about the power of socialising via the connectivity inherent to the medium and making that work for your business.

Further Reading and References:

Dell can be found at http://dell.com/.

CNN can be found at http://cnn.com/.

URL shortening services:

http://tinyurl.com/

http://is.gd/

http://bit.ly/

Official Wire: ***Building Communities In Social Media Is A Full-Time Job*** by Lawrence Perry found at:

http://www.officialwire.com/

Is your social media expert really an expert? by Peter Shankman and Sarah Evans – found at:

http://shankman.com/is-your-social-media-expert-really-an-expert/

Communicating effectively, 140 Characters at a Time by Greg Henderson – Found at:

http://www.hopeoutloud.com/blog/post/ Communicating-effectively-140-Characters-at-a-Time.aspx

Mashing it up: Nicolas Carr on Twitter's 140 Character Limit found at:

http://smasie.blogspot.com/2009/11/nicholas-carr-on-twitters-140-character.html

Section 1

What is Social Media?

Understanding Social Media

Is social media changing the world today? No, it is the people who are leveraging this technological platform to communicate in more imaginative ways than ever before. It is giving people an ability to express themselves in creative new ways. It is how people use technology that is changing the world today. Going on a trip to Paris? Want to get recommendations for a good hotel, restaurants, night spot, etc?

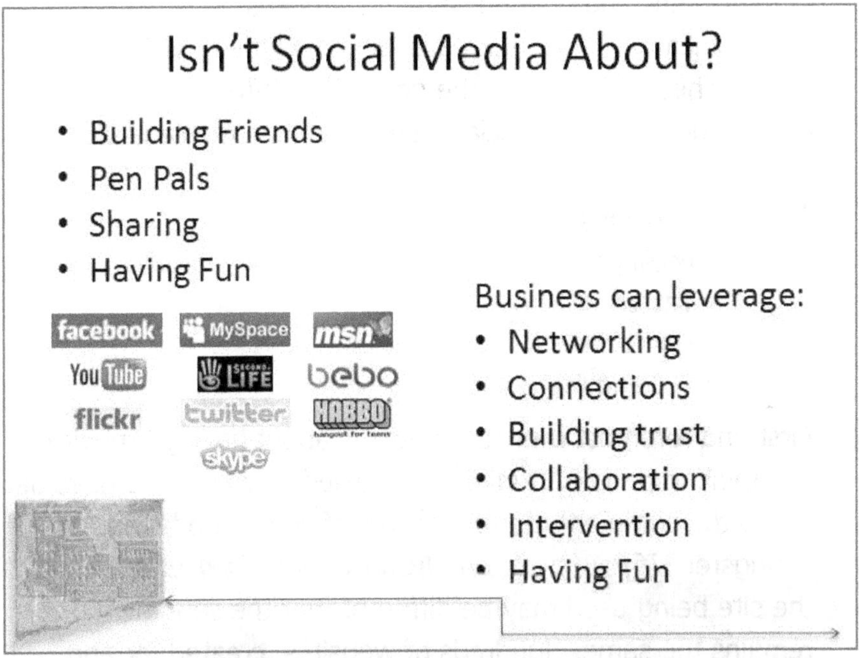
Isn't Social Media About?
• Building Friends
• Pen Pals
• Sharing
• Having Fun
facebook
MySpace
msn
YouTube
SECOND LIFE
bebo
flickr
twitter
HABBO
skype
Business can leverage:
• Networking
• Connections
• Building trust
• Collaboration
• Intervention
• Having Fun

With traditional directories you can find information after you arrive. You could ask the hotel concierge, but you probably don't know them either and the place they recommend is as likely to belong to their friend or relative, rather than be somewhere good. A network connection is likely to be able to give much better advice, and hey they may even be available to meet you and show you some of the highlights of the city if they happen to live locally.

There is both a personal and a business side to the media.

Personal Context

Almost the first aspect of this newly developing media that hit the streets was the way that it was being used by those in their teens and twenties as a new means of communication, that their parents know little or nothing about. These youth were the generation after text messaging. From the social aspect this new media is all about:

- Thoughts
- Feelings
- Tastes
- Preferences
- Building friendships

First and foremost this new media is about having fun with like-minded people. It initially appealed to youth. We have all heard the comment made a couple of years ago by one youngster "*If you're not on MySpace, you don't exist*". Today the site being used may be different, but the sentiment remains the same. Hundreds of websites, created for and often by young people, encourage and facilitate youth involvement in everything from voting, to school and community improvement, to journalism, to political activism, music selection any anything else you care to think of. Yet it is a different style of involvement than many other people think of. Taken together, they constitute an emerging genre on the Internet that could loosely be called e-citizens. What is interesting about e-citizenship is that it has rapidly become a global community. If Facebook were a nation it would currently be the third largest nation with over 400 million members.

So much has changed in the modern world and social media is responsible for part of it. It is the equivalent of building an on-line version of the pen-pals of yesteryear. The only difference being that with social media you tend to build more lasting relationships, not give up your pen-pals as most of us did when we left school. It can be argued that the relationships we are building through social media can be the strongest we will ever have. There is a certain rush from being able to help someone on the other side of the planet in some tiny way.

The important aspect here is that whatever your personal aims, goals, aspirations, likes, dislikes, political views, religious views there is probably a site waiting for you to join right now. As a medium Social Media is so broad that for any person it can be 'what you want it to be'. You don't get that with a newspaper, or with television.

On Facebook the largest user community is, and has always been 18 to 25 year olds. Some of the things teens have done include:

- Complain about teachers (or make fun of them)
- Made fun of other students
- Share intimate personal details or thoughts
- Created a fake identity or persona

- Used their friend's account to post something without them knowing
- Pretended to be an adult
- Downloaded illegal files (e.g. music, or video)
- Posted something they later regret

But consider many supposedly responsible adults have also done much the same thing, including complaining about their boss or colleagues and pretend to be a child. Like their child counterparts they also do plenty of things they later regret. There has been dramatic growth in all age ranges on Facebook, particularly each of the age groups over 40. Retirees are reconnecting with old friends. While many that are in their 40's and 50's are finding it a useful professional networking tool. There is still an element of fun, but now with a large dose of professionalism.

Discussing social media with a college professor recently showed how social media is impacting much of what we do. He no longer gives any of students his biographical information, he simply encourages them to Google him then discuss in class. Furthermore he also watches the social media space in order to know what is being said about himself and through this finds ways to improve how he delivers his lectures.

Every person right from when we first learn to talk till the day we die has their own thoughts, feelings, tastes, preferences, values, friends, circle of influence, loves to share, and wants to have fun. These are things we do in our personal lives and have done for many generations. Sure definitions of 'fun' may change from generation to generation, and from location to location. Change is inevitable and as a society we simply deal with it and adapt to the new technologies. If we look back to the mass introduction of the telephone it was both a useful tool for personal communications children could talk with their grand-parents continents away for the first time. The mobile (or cellular) phone brought its own challenges and benefits. Today they are a part of our every day lives - we simply use them wherever we are.

The point about social media is that it is bringing like-minded people together from around the world in a way that the telephone did not. It breaks through the limits of the phone system, keeping all friends updated at the same time. It is a place for the cheer-leaders and the football jock to hang out as well as the Goths and all the other cliques that can be found in any high-school. Knowing another person's phone number or email address is not necessary in order to connect with them. Whether this is a good thing or a bad thing is immaterial as it is a fact of life today, as are the business opportunities that can be garnered from such a media.

The key aspect here is about building a community. Business can be as much a part of that community as any individual. If you have products that your target audience are interested in then there is every reason to be taking part in this arena. The music industry has for many year had its eyes and ears open in the streets listening for the thoughts and feelings of its consumers and listening out for talent to match. The latest buzz on the music scene is now being talked about on Twitter, Facebook and other sites. The record companies may even be able to find demos on-line for many upcoming artists.

It is about building communities. These communities may start as social and move into the business realm (as Facebook has) or may primarily be business focused but have plenty of social opportunities (one couple who met on LinkedIn have subsequently tied the knot, getting married in a superb ceremony).

It must always be remembered that humans are essentially social animals, it is what drives us. We have all heard and laughed at the saying "I work to enjoy my life" for many having fun is an important aspect of their life. Part of being that 'social animal' we prefer to associate with people who are like ourselves. It is about interacting, and opening up your persona a little, yet still stay safe behind the computer screen. Yet at the same time this media has brought us some compelling news stories from the people directly affected e.g. the recent spate of earthquakes around the world where dramatic pictures were relayed on Twitter instantly.

This brings up a question of "what exactly is personal any-more?" Sure chatting with friends is clearly personal, yet discussions on taste and choice can launch this discussion into the product realm, which is relevant to corporations with advertising money to spend, in fact the advertising that individual sees on their computer screen can be directly related to their personal focus (e.g. the TV shows talked about, perfumes, sports shoes, etc. can all be analysed and lend themselves to an instant advertising opportunity. Posting the dramatic pictures of earthquake or air-crash victims makes a person part of the news media, albeit without pay. The boundaries between personal and business are becoming increasingly blurred.

Can you have fun in the business environment? You do not need Social Media to answer this question. We all do. Psychologists have for a long time stated that people build their most important relationships in the workplace, which is probably one of the reasons why tele-communting only meets with limited success. People want to meet people and build relationships. The boundaries between social and business are blurring. Business is becoming more social (or perhaps more correctly returning to its social roots). Social Media is connection based, it is about people helping people - and this is the basis of human society. Ultimately the social and business goals for this media are not so far apart.

The Challenge for Business - Relationship Based Business

Business is constantly changing and reinventing itself. The author spoke at an event recently about growing relationship based businesses. The initial thinking of this subject was summed up in the question: "*Isn't every business is relationship based?*"

Yes it is; you have no sales without having a basic relationship with a customer. In defining what a 'Relationship Based Business' was the author came to the conclusion it is:

> *Ensuring a successful relationship, through communication and collaboration embodying a value based approach in order to win business.*

Perhaps in growing the modern mega corporation we have lost focus on the relationship aspect of building the business. Modern business demands the ability to maximise value to customers as well as a way to drive additional revenue from them; we achieve this through managing the relationship and building partnerships.

Customer relationship management (CRM) has long been on the agenda for business growth - yet to many this is merely an IT system rather than an essential way of life for the organisation. With Social Media there is a need for a more holistic customer relationship management process. We talk to customers and prospects, we address their concerns while building a relationship with them in a public forum. The relationship we build is not one-to-one, it is based on the needs of one individual but it is visible to a much broader audience.

There is an old maxim that we hold our friends close and our enemies even closer. In social-media-land it is important to build relationships with your customers and with prospects alike - the reasons are obvious. We also need to build relationships with competitors - why? To know what they are saying and doing. Then there are a wealth of other people that we need to build relationships with, including researchers, writers, industry experts, shipping companies, suppliers, etc, etc. Social media impacts them all.

Ultimately there is a sphere of influence that extends beyond the organisation and its staff. This must by its public nature extend to the industry at large; it is like everything that we do being published in a trade journal for all to see.

Generally improving business visibility is good, we all want that - it drives in fresh business. Dell has stated that it expects to have sales of over $6 million through its activity in Social Media channels in 2010. This level of sales comes about through a commitment to direct marketing and Social Media that operates worldwide across the company. It comes from building trust as market experts in the area of Windows and PC faults etc. and not just from Dell customers. Dell takes an approach that ensure responses are made by people with the real knowledge - it is more likely to be the product designer than a advertising person because they do not want to have a 'promotional spin' put on the story. To them the response must be focused, accurate and deliver knowledge to the person needing it. This delivers VALUE to the customer, or prospect, or indeed to anyone who may care to read the contribution provided.

An open dialogue wins friends, not only is the person with the problem impressed that a mega-corporation took the time to respond, but they did so in a timely and accurate manner, even when the question related to another company's product. For Dell this pays dividends because that person will add the company to their shortlist when they are looking for a new product that Dell sells - Dell will be on the shortlist. The other aspect about this dialogue is that it is public.

Yet there is also a negative side to all of this visibility: failures can be seen by all as clearly as successes. Again though this needs to be managed in an open and honest way. Businesses are driven by people and as we all know people do make mistakes. Faults must be managed, business needs an intelligent intervention in the Social Media space to understand what is being said about all brands owned and to respond appropriately.

> *BUT! Asks one Sales Executive, surely the reason I want my business to be using Social Media is to sell more products?*

Yes, very true. Yet as discussed before moving traditional 'push-based' advertising techniques into the social media world does not guarantee sales success. Your business can advertise on social media sites, it can even be targeted to appeal to specific audiences, but remember more than ever before people have learned to tune-out advertising on web sites - when they have a purpose, a goal, responding to that advert no matter how compelling the message will mean they delay or never reach their goal. Involvement in Social Media means more than simply advertising, it means being involved.

Obviously revenue is important, we could not survive long in business without it. However it is closely bound together in a relationship based business. Part of selling is providing a solution for other people's problems. We are better able to provide solutions by understanding those problems; listening; asking questions; building relationships; envisioning solutions. This is at the heart of a social media engagement. In addition developing a market intelligence can ensure we understand our customers needs better.

It may be that building sales through trusted relationship takes a longer sales cycle, but yet people may also be lining up at your door because of your social media intervention.

Some sales take more patience than others but then you are adding value through every communication in an holistic way. One of the longer term results will be increasing customer loyalty around specific products - something that has been lacking of late in certain industry sectors. In fact brand loyalty can be put back on the agenda through correct use of Social Media.

A New World of Business Networking

In investigating the business benefit gained by adopting collaborative technologies within the workplace it was concluded that whilst there were significant benefits they would only be viable in certain types of business or situation. As time has moved on this thinking has changed. Business networking, collaborative technologies, web 2.0, and Enterprise 2.0, are a necessary part of the changing business landscape. Having been through very tough times, it is the business that adapts best to the new world is the most likely to survive.

Why Business Networking?

We have seen a significant rise in the use of Social Networking. According to compete.com usage of all of the primary social networking sites has been growing for some time:

- ◊ LinkedIn 13 million users per month.
- ◊ Facebook 120 million users.
- ◊ YouTube 103 million users.
- ◊ Twitter 28 million monthly users.

- ◊ Myspace 68 million users
- ◊ Windows Live 68 million users

It should be noted that while each of these sites claim larger membership compete.com is only measuring actual visits, e.g. the active membership. Please remember each of these has a part to play in developing how any business leverages the social web. In developing the Internet we have moved from few contributors and a large set of spectators to a growing world of writers and commentators. The internet space is being democratised. With that old relationships are changing. The Internet has become a way to say anything that you want to say. In the section called "How to Leverage the Social Media Channel for Business Success" this book discusses a new attitude that needs to be adopted in business. One of the key concepts of networking is that you must give in order to receive. This applies to social media marketing techniques.

The rising world of business networking is one that adopts new techniques in order to build trust and win business. This however demands giving something of value in order to get something of greater value. Be willing to assist a prospect solve a problem (without charge) in order to secure them as a client. This has many parallels to social use of the new media except that the individual concerned is not watching out for Auntie Mavis' latest update on her world tour, the corporation is looking at building connections based on common goals and capabilities.

Not about the Technology

Think about this:

- It is about people making connections
- We know "People like people like themselves"
- Technology is just a connector
- Social Networking becomes a "Stepping-Stone" for business

The technology facilitates an ability to connect, nothing more. The sites used to make connections are not important, in fact we should be making use of many different social media channels to explore different types of connection.

Technology Foundation

For a technologist to suggest that the technology is not important may seem like heresy, but it is not. What is important is how you leverage any site for your business aims. Traditionally we would spend a lot of time investigating capability and the viability of solution providers. With social media it is always advisable to build a multi-channel approach. You are using technology owned by another organisation and simply do not know how that channel will change in the future.

Whilst talking about financial viability, let as take the example of Twitter, much has been made out of the fact that the site makes no income. Yet the company does have a solid venture capital foundation. If you were purchasing software from such a company then this may be of concern, but here you are merely leveraging its ability to deliver messages on your behalf, an ability to communicate that is all. It is also important to have a presence on multiple communities; particularly those having relevance to your marketplace.

In this regard sites do crash from time to time and they always seem to do so the most inconvenient of times. When this happens wait a couple of hours before returning to the site, normally the issues will have been resolved.

Any corporation should adopt a multi-vendor approach. Having a Facebook fan page as well as a Twitter account is an essential part of a multi-faceted Social Media approach. Leveraging multiple vendors acts as an insurance policy, should any individual channel go out of business or change its focus then your business simply adapts to the new reality and moves on to a more appropriate channel, and you do not have to build a fresh following if you are already present on the site. The future of Social Media sites is one of growth, both in terms of demographic focus and in terms of interest groups.

There is likely to also be a growth in specialist sites that have 'social' capabilities for example trade journals or trade associations. During the course of investigations the author has identified IT, accounting, marketing and other communities that are build on social involvement. Volunteer organisations, trade associations and trade unions all have sites that aimed at knowledge sharing and furthering that organisation's aims and to connect members.

Leveraging Connections

There are several key aspects to learn about Social Media; these include the fact that Social Media should not be viewed as a technological challenge, but a people challenge; albeit founded on technology; BUT it is all about connections and how you leverage them.

> *Two-thirds of marketing professionals... consider themselves 'very knowledgeable' or 'somewhat knowledgeable' about (social media marketing) emerging strategy.*
>
> http://marketingsherpa.com/ April 14th 2009

Marketing Sherpa went on to note that they felt very few advertising professionals were really comfortable about leveraging the new media successfully and that:

◊ Social Media is different from traditional advertising!

◊ New skills & new technologies are involved

While technology is the foundation the largest element of this revolution is entirely personal in nature. To succeed leveraging this new we must be able to communicate effectively and network effectively. At the end of the day networking still requires people in order to make connections. Business builds from those connections. The medium merely facilitates that ability to make connections with people we would not otherwise be able to contact. It allows this to happen in a relatively safe way as there is no need to give out email addresses or personal contact details if you are not comfortable doing so.

Do not be afraid to connect with people. According to recent research 75% of all Twitter users have less than 10 followers. This is all the more surprising since many non-celebrities have more than a million connections on the site. One of the key aspects about Twitter and other social media sites is that you do not need to provide any person with your email address, phone number, or street address in order to communicate with them. Indeed it is possible to stay entirely anonymous other than the details provided in your bio.

You can find the author on Twitter at @pgiblett and if he does not wish to tell you other contact details then that is all you need to know to communicate effectively. Yet at the same time it is possible to talk about business opportunities, jobs, or anything else that is relevant in respect of the relationship built. Plenty of business opportunities or jobs exist through LinkedIn, Twitter and other communities. The social web can be great for driving interest to your product.

In terms of on-line activity, here are some things that are worth thinking about:

- "I am off to the cinema now" type communications are not *normally* relevant.
- 99.999+% of everything on the internet is of no relevance whatsoever to what you are working on right now.
- Networking is merely a means to extend the scope of what you are working by involving others.
- The people on your personal 'A-list' warrant special attention.
- Replies always need personal attention

For professional networking answering Twitter's question "**What's happening?**" is normally the worst way to use the site. Facebook's "**What is on your mind?**" is probably closer to the truth. But the professional networker is really on the site to "**Tell the world something of significance**", although it could also be "**Tell the world something of value**". At the end of the day everything you say is visible to the world and should offer value to your marketplace. Blogs are the darlings of the search engines as they provide gigabytes of new content every day to be analysed and combine well with social media to communicate value. Twitter is one mechanism to driving people towards your message and it is pretty effective at doing just that.

The question "What's happening?" should not be answered unless you are telling people in an active conversation that you are no longer available (e.g. you have gone to a meeting). Your reason for being on social media is twofold: to promote what you are doing; and to intervene in the marketplace. Revenue opportunities do exist, but they will come in the course of your other activity. Don't expect Social Media be become an instant money making machine.

This is your opportunity to promote things you are working on, including corporate blog posts, forum discussions and everything else the company is doing. Every message you send should be:

- Up-to-date
- Relevant
- and provide real value

Building connections is one method that can help in getting your message out. Not every person you connect with is interested in your product today, but they may be tomorrow. The reason for building a wide set of connections is about demonstrating expertise in the marketplace. A must for connections are customers and the people who work for them. If you can find a prospect you are currently talking to then connect with them.

The "Anyone interested in your product" can be quite a wide net to cast, however if you are a realtor in Queens then you are interested in connecting with anyone in New York to start with as they may be interested in the properties you have for sale. When people follow you think about whether you can potentially help them, if you can then follow back.

In following back you are not interested in people offering naughty naked pictures of themselves, those pushing MLM schemes, or those pointing you at sites where you can make astonishing wealth. These folk are not interested in your message, besides the reason for you presence is for professional branding. They are simply interested in leveraging the social web for modern spam, junk mail (or in this case junk posts) as an issue is not going to disappear simply because we have shifted media. You will end up with some who befriend you – please do remember that you can always un-friend them or block them if they become a nuisance.

A final word on following. Get connected. Don't be afraid of followers, they cannot get to you unless you give them your personal details. If you do decide to give out your details then only do so via a Personal or Direct Message – where you can be sure that you are talking on a one-to-one basis.

Further Reading and References:

"Why Youth (Heart) Social Network Sites" by Danah Boyd at:

http://www.danah.org/papers/WhyYouthHeart.pdf

"Youth as E-Citizens Engaging the Digital Generation" by Centre for Social Media found at:

http://www.centerforsocialmedia.org/future-public-media/documents/articles/youth-e-citizens-engaging-digital-generation

"Cliques" by MassGeneral Hospital for Children at:

http://www.massgeneral.org/children/adolescenthealth/articles/aa_cliques.aspx

"Is Telecommuting the best model for future business?" by Peter Giblett is found at:

http://cio-perspectives.com/2008/12/is-telecommuting-the-best-model-for-future-business/

Does Business Require an Holistic Approach to Marketing? By Peter B. Giblett can be found at:

http://cio-perspectives.com/2009/11/does-business-require-an-holistic-approach-to-marketing/

Section 2

What does Social Media do for my business?

Social Media: A Revolution?

How many times have we heard the term 'revolution' applied to things in business? We have probably heard the term used more frequently than we care to remember.

A revolution should mean something that brings a significant advance, for business this is normally measured in terms of revenue generation or capabilities. Understanding Social Media takes a big shift in entrenched thinking is required in order for marketing to fully exploit the capabilities of social media.

While advertising agencies can help design campaigns they are unable to put you in touch with the key influencers in your own marketplace. For many businesses these actually come from the combined personal network of connections of their key employees. This is one of the challenges social networking brings. Yet advertising agencies can still add value to the process, through building the publicity and campaign material – the message that drives to the heart of the business and its ability to deliver.

From a recruitment viewpoint networking has always been key to adding senior staff. With the aid of social media that network can stretch much further. Social media adds significant value to the recruitment process across right from the electrician to the CEO. Social networks are also great places to engage industry experts, discuss challenges, identify solutions. One aspect to be considered is that much of the material comes at no cost, other than time.

A couple of challenges:

- "Everyone else is doing it!" and
- "it seems like I am the late to the party"

One business owner complained recently of precisely these concerns.

Usually "every else is doing it" is the single worst excuse to do anything in business. It is true that the world is changing and it is true that your business needs to be part of that change, but more important than simply jumping in to social media is gaining an understanding of how it functions and developing the policies and procedures necessary to make it work correctly for your business.

To be clear there is no such thing as being "late to the party" and it is vital that every business must proceed at its own pace. Yes, there is considerable pressure to socialise your business but whether it is right to do so will depend on the nature of the industry and competitive pressure.

It is better to understand the nature of the problem before jumping in with guns blazing. Understand whether changes need to be made to your business model, your business processes, your web-site before getting going. However you get involved in social media you have to think about collaboration and your market intervention in order to build connections or 'friends'. Unless you are a star of the silver screen or a global brand name it will not be possible to build a large group of listeners overnight.

Some thoughts:

Involvement requires listening to customers.

Build relationships with all that are interested in your marketplace

Involvement requires building a listening organisation.

Involvement means building a social media intelligence for your marketplace.

Look out for people mention your product, brand, company, etc.

Build a dialogue with them.

Talk to all people in your marketplace.

Help to fix other people's problems.

Each area requires constant attention. Yet generally responses made do not have to be instant, but they do need to be timely. It is acceptable to be aware of what is being said and respond within a few hours. A key reason never to post an instant response – how many times have you lived to regret the instant email response? Usually a little time reveals a much better answer Spelling and good grammar are always important. Yet the message should not be one invented by a slick advertising person – it has to be genuine and responsive going to the heart of the matter.

To give you a flavour of Social Media, remember there are a lot of sites with a lot of specialities. When you have some time then look up some of these sites on Google and think whether they have any relevance to growing your business.

This list given here shows a small sample of the total number of sites that exist today. These seem to specialise in:

1. Personal networking
2. Business networking
3. Communication
4. Collaboration
5. Personal development
6. Knowledge Sharing

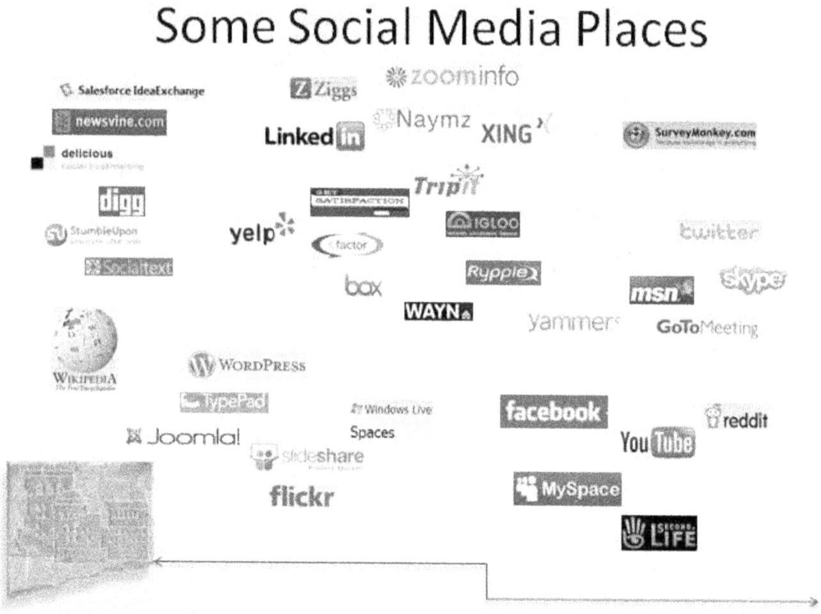

Currently there are more than 800 sites offering a variety of services in the social media space today, the marketplace is growing and new sites are being added daily. It would not be possible to put together a single picture of all the sites that exist. Please remember that NOT ALL WILL SURVIVE, particularly when you have a highly specialised focus area. Additionally new, as yet unheard of sites may come to the fore in specialist areas.

The Social Landscape

This brief look at the some of the social media landscape is taken from the product branding perspective:

Website	Customer Communication	Brand Exposure	Driving Traffic to Your Website
Twitter	Good for engaging people who are discussing your brand. Be involved in the ongoing conversation to win converts.	Lots of potential to make your brand visible and to engage interested people. Avoid direct advertising though.	Lots of opportunity to link to your brand's web site, but best in leveraging a blog rather than an advertising type of site.
Facebook	Great for engaging people. Share your brand views through a fan page. Potential for prizes and contests.	Great for brand exposure, you can enhance social exposure by traditional advertising.	Traffic to your site can be limiting except to a blog post.
LinkedIn	Not the primary focus. There are opportunities to engage by answering questions and establishing expertise	Good for personal branding, must not be used for corporate branding. Employees should be encouraged to have powerful profiles and be active.	Unlikely to drive any significant traffic to your site. Involvement in Answers can pay dividends though.
YouTube	A good place to add informative videos. Can be a good	A very powerful branding tool, but please avoid using	The affect is secondary as traffic goes to

	place to engage customers links to Twitter etc.	it for 'TV' style adverts – people want to be informed, build infomercials instead.	the videos not to your site. Can add links in descriptions, but does not bring much traffic.
MySpace	Once the leader, now lagging behind. Opportunities for engagement still exist. Needs to be focused though.	Opportunities still exist. Best to ensure MySpace posts are automatically though other services like ping.fm.	Unlikely to drive any significant traffic to your site. Involvement is key.
Windows Live	Opportunities for engagement do exist. Involvement needs to be focused though as the site has not reached its full potential.	Primarily for personal branding, should not be used for corporate branding.	Unlikely to drive any significant traffic to your site.
Flikr	Primarily a photo sharing site. Proper photo tags are important to allow customers to see the people behind your brand.	Not particularly helpful in building brand awareness. Photos not linked to brand or blog.	Poor click through rates generally. Can drive some interest for 'famous brands'.
Digg	Powerful if the customer favourites you, but limited otherwise. Good marks can positively impact page ranking.	Lots of potential for good exposure provided customers care about the things you offer.	Can provide a lot of traffic. This tends to work best for non-commercial blogs rather than normal corporate web sites. Links

			well to other social tools.
Stumble Upon	Powerful if the customer bookmarks you. Good remarks can positively impact page ranking.	Lots of potential for good exposure when people care about the things offered on your site. Offers paid campaigns.	Enables discovery from a diverse audience. Can provide a lot of traffic whenever there is a buzz about your product.

Why Should we Use Social Media in Our Business?

Some of the pundits in the social media marketing field seem to be in the panic business. You have probably heard some who are saying that if you are not leveraging Social Media today then your business is doomed to fail. This is simply not true. It is more important to focus on how to correctly leverage this media. Recognise that each business has to make their own decisions about adoption, and should not be influenced by the adoption hype. Make the move at a time that is right for your business.

A business that is making products focused on the teen and twenties market will almost certainly need to be thinking about social media as a key part of their marketing communication plans. Without it they are probably not reaching all of their key buyers. On the other hand a local auto repair business may see little sense in using social media as a part of their communication mix. However rarely are things so clear cut.

Perhaps the local auto repair mechanic has simply not considered what social media can do for his business. He puts adverts for his business into the local Yellow Pages, or the local newspaper. This brings him business. The other aspect that brings business is through personal recommendations. One neighbour asks another for a good local mechanic. This system is similar to the relationships of trust built within social media. When the mechanic understands the value this media bring his business then he will see it as essential to leverage the media.

Things are not quite as clear cut as some would like them to be. Social Media is one of many mechanisms the any business can leverage to bring in new business. This chapter continues to investigate this question.

12 Questions you Should Ask.

One of the biggest challenges when a new technology comes along is in understanding its business impact. In this regard Social Media is no different to other technologies in this regard. Here are the top questions a business leader should ask when defining their Social Media intervention:

- ◊ Where do I find my customers, or prospects?
- ◊ How can our customers help us grow our business?
- ◊ How is our marketplace changing?
- ◊ Who should we be learning from?
- ◊ How do we make money using these new channels?
- ◊ What will our audience be on these new channels?
- ◊ What new things should we provide to support the Social Media Channel?
- ◊ How do we demonstrate our reputation as the best in the business?
- ◊ How do we extend our business network?
- ◊ There are so many sites out there which ones should we be using? And how?

◊ How do we know if our efforts are working?
◊ Who is doing it well and how are they doing it?

Many consider Social Media as something their children, or grandchildren, use and not for hard core business. There is an understanding that this new media is about our youth and their buddies. How can this possibly have a business impact?

We have discussed how social media is about: thoughts and feelings; tastes and preferences; building friends and pen-pals; social values; sharing music and videos; having fun. What possible interest could this be to business? Especially since we are not going to allow people to use SecondLife, Flickr, or YouTube at work, are we? Actually when executed properly business can leverage the social media channels to bring an increasing return. This involves: making connections; building a network; building trust; collaboration; image management; being involved in marketplace discussions; and having fun.

Yes it is possible to associate business with having fun. Leveraging social media channels is different from traditional advertising. Social media is available to all age ranges including the retired community. New skills are involved, but this is not about technology. It is about people connecting with people. The technological layer simply provides the mechanism to make the connection between two people.

People like others that think the same way as they do. With technology as the connector it is possible to get a prospect referral that is located down the street by someone on the other side of the planet. The world is changing, yet doing business is as much about who we know as about what we know. That is building business relationships. These channels are becoming the stepping-stone for new business. At the end of the day collaboration and intervention in marketplace discussions are the foundation to making money in the social media world.

CEO Clinic:

Why do we need Social Media?

One CEO recently asked "What is in it for me and I suppose that means more expenditure?" His thinking: business has to know the value of every investment. Having discussed his concerns it was possible to identify some key areas for improvements within the business including communications and collaboration within the company and the tools they used for communications. So of course we came to the inevitable question "***How does Social Media improve communications?***" This is such an important question because it focuses on one of the core aspects of the new media.

Social media allows any corporation, irrespective of its size to be involved in the world market for their specialist segment. Involvement in Social Media is about connecting to both people and businesses. Who do you connect with? Customers, obviously as we wish to maintain and enhance your ongoing relationship with them, suppliers

– likewise they are a vital part of your extended business realm. Prospects, of course, are necessary to grow the business. Competitors – Excuse me, you cannot be serious? Of course we know the old maxim about holding your friends close and your enemies closer – well it applies to Social Media as much as in any other medium.

However involvement in the medium is in itself not sufficient – it is important to have a strategy for successful intervention. Without a strategy your intervention is doomed to failure, somewhat akin to chasing the latest greatest gadget as there will always be another one coming very soon. Of course there is no problem with companies jumping onto a social media site, e.g. Twitter, just to try it out, but it is important to define what you wish to accomplish, even if you are just defining one or two goals. If you are looking to drive additional sales for example how are you going to measure:

1) the additional traffic, and
2) the sales uplift?

Taking a little time is important and will tend to accomplish much more. Now of course we cannot tell what was in the mind of the purchaser when they saw a specific Twitter posting, but nonetheless they will come and some will purchase.

"So you are talking about extending my advertising strategy?" asked the curious CEO. Well the answer of course is both yes and no. You can advertise in the various Social Media channels, like Facebook, MSN, or LinkedIn, and you can even target your message so that it appeals to *specific* demographic sectors (e.g. one ad for teens and another for mothers) but that is not leveraging the real power Social Media provides which is more about creating a dialogue with those that can be interested in your business or its products/services.

Crucially involvement is more about communication and intervening in the chatter happening about your marketplace. There is no question that when people are talking about your products, your brands, your company then the business needs to be on the pulse and needs to responding appropriately. When people praise you it is always essential to thank them (you may also wish to consider asking to connect with them). Many times praise may extend as far as providing discount vouchers or other promotions.

When people criticise you it is even more essential to respond appropriately and in a timely manner, in fact intervention it is even more crucial at this time than when your business is being praised. The best tactic is to face any problem head-on, do not attempt to bribe people. Gifts and promotions tend to be seen as an attempt to buyout the critic. They may go away, but the action can be seen as unethical. It is better to try to create a dialogue with that person in private (either via a direct message or preferably via the phone). Some people need their grievances to be aired in public so a genuine responses are crucial.

Every person and every company does things wrong from time to time. Normally honesty brings more kudos when things go wrong – the same rule exists in social media land. Someone once made the analogy that business relationships on social media are more akin to the personal relationship built with the corner store your grandparents once used. Well if managed right any commercial business dealings can be built on a relationship of trust.

The other aspect of building an intervention strategy is in knowing what is being said about your marketplace. No matter your business there is already someone blogging , or using YouTube, or have created a podcast. It is important to manage your digital footprint. You need to have a blog in addition to your website. The website is focused around selling your products or services whereas you blog is about adding value to the marketplace.

The blog can have a multitude of articles, including how to use your products, installation advice, and other frequently asked questions as well as commentary on the marketplace, critiques of products etc. If you do decide to critique products then ensure you add links to web sites and it is important be fair about the genuine state of the market. Also you should link to interesting articles by industry experts, particularly those relating to future trends.

"You are telling us to change our whole marketing approach?" some pundits will claim that if people cannot find you online (especially in social media channels) then you are invisible. This is NOT true for every business, for some Yellow Pages is still an essential part of their promotional activities – where do you turn when you need Auto Repair

Shop, or Lawyer? Yes Yellow pages! Yet social media can be a crucial differentiator. This is where a balanced approach is required – one thing is sure involvement in social media, provided these guidelines are followed will ensure that you do have a favourable presence.

Marketing Case Study: A Matter of Time

Along with a wide list of business owners Jill McLaren had no interest in Twitter, or any other Social Media technology. The closest she ever came to the media was an email message from her niece inviting her to MySpace a few years ago – thinking to herself that there were many other ways to communicate with the young family member she simply binned the invite and got on with her life.

She owned a small Specialist Engineering company that she inherited from her uncle a few years ago. This was a true family business, with most of her cousins being involved at some time during their careers. Sadly during the recession in 2008 one of her largest clients collapsed unable to pay their debts, including $20,000 worth of equipment McLaren's company had just completed manufacturing. To have any hope of recovering this money they had find alternative buyers.

She was looking for any perspective buyer, including talking to other customers. Spending was down across all her customers and none of them was about to buy equipment that did not fit their specifications. By chance she mentioned her problem to a friend with a public relations background who suggested looking on Twitter for people in her field.

Not knowing what Twitter was McLaren investigated further. She could see that the service was growing phenomenally, just under 2000% in 2008 and 1200% in 2009. The place to start was perhaps Twitter's "Search" tool. To her surprise there was an active discussion in her marketplace, she also found many customers and prospect that were already using the service. Furthermore she found that they were looking for solutions to their problems, answers she could easily provide, but did not know where to begin doing so.

Her PR friend suggested that publishing a blog may be the thing to do. In the meanwhile McLaren had already started responding to the questions raised on Twitter giving advice in snippets in 140 characters. Within days her following grew from nothing to several hundred, and now exceeds two thousand. During the course of her discussions she posted between 5 to 10 messages per day. Fast forward a few weeks and her blog site had been setup she answered many of the questions in more detail. She tied the twitter questions to her blog posts and found that within weeks her blog was attracting an independent following.

Thanks to Twitter and Blog posts she now receives enquiries for new business each week. She never did find a buyer for the equipment she was trying to sell, but the business has more than made up for the loss by the value of the new clients obtained, with the order books being full. McLaren now spends about 5 or 6 hours a week on Twitter or creating new blog posts. It is paying its weight in gold, yes they still advertise in Yellow Pages, and the trade journals but it is through Twitter that customers are seeing the true value her company provides to the marketplace. They are coming to trust this little family business as one of the leaders. The cost → nothing but time!

Furthermore she is seen as a trusted advisor in her marketplace and has been invited to speak at a symposium later in the year.

Further Reading and References:

"Social Media for CEOs" by Mitch Joel is found at:

http://www.canadianbusiness.com/entrepreneur/sales_marketing/article.jsp?content=20090901_30012_30012

Some of the Rules of Social Media

There are plenty of rules that have been written about social media. One of the key ones is to be polite and to thank people whenever they do you a favour. This is especially important if you represent a global mega corporation. Hey this is just like real life! Remember there are a lot of people out there, each with their own goals and objectives. If someone helps you it is because for a fleeting moment your objectives were aligned – it does not mean they will do it again tomorrow.

Rules of Social Networking for Business

- Social Networking is a dialogue
- Be real
- Offer something of value
- Be a resource & participate
- Know your target audience
- Create content
- Be fresh
- Learn to say "NO!"
- 'Let go' of an idea – let others develop/own it
- Have FUN!

If you search this subject on Google you will probably come up with over 2000 rules, so this is just a starting point. The key is participation and being genuine.

There are a few points to consider, which are covered in the remainder of this chapter.

Good Manners Must Always be in Style!

A business partner posed a question about Social Media etiquette: "What do you do when a valued customer uses bad language on a Social Media channel?"

The trouble is that when something is said on the Internet it tends to stay around for quite a while. There is no call for bad language on any platform. The author has blocked Twitter followers for persistent use of bad language, but then again they are not customers. So what do we do if customers or suppliers use bad language? What comes first to mind is education. Everyone needs to be reminded about the longevity of statements made on the web and that bad language shows a disrespect to those in their community.

Jennifer Laycock in "Dear Miss Social Media Manners..." gives several pointers, including:

- Be nice
- Be respectful
- Apologize when you make mistakes
- Say "thank you"

The last of these does have to be learnt by the participant. Laura Lake in *Mind Your Manners* states "It's true you will not find a list of dos and don'ts when it comes to social media marketing, but you must mind your manners in order for your efforts... to be successful" and "If you approach social media without paying attention to proper etiquette you could be seen as… lack[ing] respect and possess[ing] bad manners".

Even the Trump Blog asks "Are good manners out of style?" and Thomas M. Schmitz comments "Some people are friendly and polite with their buddies, family, colleagues and co-workers. But when it comes to people that they do not know, like baristas, store clerks and servers, they remain dispassionate, neither mean nor nice". It has become a natural form of behaviour but is essential that everyone take time to think about how that is wrong and have reform their behaviour.

In "Twelve Important Social Marketing Manners" Cynthia Nowicki advises that we all should "Think things out before hitting the submit or send button – is there anyone that might react poorly to what you are about to send? Take a breather and have someone else review your message before sending". That is the difference between creating blogs and publishing in a newspaper. Wait before publishing, remember it is important to "respect your audience".

"Avoid using bathroom humour" is also good advice from Nowicki. We all like to be light hearted on occasions, but remember humour cannot always be adequately communicated through a written message, especially one that only has limited formatting available. Can you really be comfortable with how other people would perceive the joke? This also stems from the fact that too many comics poke fun in directions they should not go. Ultimately there is no excuse for bad manners.

13 Rules of Twetiquette for Business

Social Media engine Twitter makes communication with others easy. Your message can be heard by a large audience. With Twitter first contact is so easy, but then it is also so easy to have people stop following you, or even after the most excessive bad behaviour block you.

Many rules have been published before. Here are the ***most important*** rules to remember and practice everyday:

1. Have a BIO – The 160 characters that says so much about the quintessential YOU.
2. Have a picture or avatar. It help us identify you. It is also best this picture is consistent with the image used on other Social Media communities.
3. Never (ever) use bad language
4. Talk business, avoid politics or religion at all times.
5. Be inventive with your 140 characters, its not much but it is so powerful.
6. Follow people in your marketplace, your customers, your prospects, your competitors and market experts.
7. Marketplace expertise – give your followers information of value through your blog.
8. Marketplace expertise – answer people's questions, become a valuable resource.

9. Multi-Level Marketing schemes are not welcome here either.
10. Unless you are associated with 'Show Business' following stars does not get you followers.
11. Be active! ONE message a week is an absolute MINIMUM. One, or more, per day is preferable.
12. The wider the group of followers you build the better. Remember it is safe. No one knows physical location unless you tell them. Give an email address only to those that you have developed a relationship with.
13. When you get followers, build relationships with people outside the social media channel. Not everyone responds those that do can become key contacts.

Twitter can be a great way of building a large number of business contacts in a short period of time. You must treat people as you expect them to treat you, with respect.

Business Networking: 30 Day Plan to Build your on-line Presence

As an aid to visualising corporate intervention in Social Media the author has put together this thirty day plan for leveraging social networks to build your business. This is a core part of getting an on-line presence established. It is probably the first thirty days that are the toughest, you are after all getting used to a strange new world. After this period it is largely about maintaining your presence, building a following, responding to people and continuing with your marketing communication and customer service activity.

1. Sign up and settle in to your chosen network
2. Set up your profile and start to define your Social Media image
3. Read around – know what others are doing
4. Connect with some people you know
5. Post something about your industry
6. Connect with some people who have a large following (super-connectors)
7. Answer a question or comment on someone's post
8. Add some more connections (find people in your own specialist area)
9. Have a little fun
10. Ask a question and interact with everyone who responds
11. Follow some of the web links people provide – understand their thinking, their likes and dislikes
12. Seek out active people (key users/evangelists) in your field
13. Communicate with active people (answer their questions, comment on their updates)
14. Find comments about your product/brand/company & categorise them
15. Identify the right way to respond to those comments
16. Do some Customer Service (and respond to the comments)
17. Post an update with a link to a web article you like (any web article)
18. Manage more questions and answers
19. Combine some on-line and off-line activities

20. Post something challenging for you and of value to connections
21. Have some fun – try some of the features you have never used before.
22. Identify another Social Media site which may is consistent with your goals
    (It is important to build a presence on multiple channels over time)
23. Drive connections to blog posts
24. Build subscriptions on you blog site – this ensures readers come back
25. Concentrate on the elements of your time-line for your second presence
26. Answer questions, debate and introduce blog posts
27. Automate some of your activities
28. Spend a little time each day looking at how to build connections
29. Update your profile, learn from others
30. Connect with people you do not know
31. Have a little more fun

In connecting with people the first port of call is your own contact list – try to find some people that you already know, you will be surprised how many people are already present.. On some sites the presence must be personal, on others a business or brand personas are permitted. Obey these rules. When connecting to people you should be looking for people in your domain of interest – don't follow stars for the sake of it as it will not affect the number who follow you.

When posting updates it is preferable you link them to a website or a blog (and this does not have to be your own in every instance – there is plenty of good material around the web). There are plenty of strategies about what to post and the frequency. Initially it is important just to make a statement to let people know you are present. Sometimes you may need to repeat a post, not word for word, but general ideas. Linking posts to blog pages is a way of adding more information than would be possible in a social media message this also adds value to your listener.

Answering questions, or commenting on someone else's contribution is important. It demonstrates your own knowledge and expertise. If your presence if brand based then the questions/comments must be relevant to the general marketplace of the brand. Build a dialogue with those who respond to your questions, this builds trust and facilitates connections.

The customer service aspects are as important a part of building on on-line presence as any media message you wish to send. Firstly seek to solve problems before seeking to sell. Try to understand people's motive for commenting on your brand, remember not everything said is a complaint. Initial analysis is important as it will determine the response given. It may seem daunting at first and hence a little planning is required. Appropriate responses will come naturally over time. Your response should never appear to be a marketing message. It is important to be honest – if there is a problem admit it and tell them when a fix is expected. Ultimately you should aim to respond quickly (within a couple of hours), but at first it is necessary to understand the best way to respond, so take your time. This is ultimately about providing an intelligent intervention.

Automation is an aspect that can be important – Every blog post written needs to be automatically posted to a number of social media sites – this informs your network that you have something new for them – this makes your publication mechanism more effective. Saying one message in multiple places can take up quite a bit of time, and automation can link a number of sites together.

Getting More from Your Social Media Profiles

In becoming active on any social media site it is your Profile that says most about you or your business to assist in making connections. It is therefore important that you pay attention and build a clear and well understood profile. There are many types of profile, including:

- ◊ Minimalist profiles – giving the barest information, their job and company.
- ◊ Maximalist profiles that use every character of space that can be used in each section.

Ironically both approaches are wrong. A social media profile should assist a visitor in deciding whether you are a person they may wish to build some form of relationship with.

Let us be clear before we go a step further. Sites like LinkedIn are NOT purely for job hunters, they are sites that professionals use to build professional connections. Yes a percentage of the population are currently seeking a job. Other members of the community are also building business connections. Whatever your current aim social media sites like LinkedIn and Facebook are here to stay and will be a part of a professional's portfolio well into the future. The job-hunter of today will become the sales manager of tomorrow and will always leverage their Social Media network as a business tool.

The profile should most of all be professional, and it should headline your capabilities and achievements in a way that invites people to want to know you. You need to use your social media profiles consistently with what you are looking to get out of the medium. You should look to have a consistent profile across a range of social networks, yet focus on the specific needs of the site in question.

Where possible link your profile to both your personal blog or website. This will allow a connection to have as complete a picture of you as possible. Please ensure you update the information on your profile when you move jobs or change your focus.

So what is your name? Of course know you know what your name is, but consistency is key. Some connections of mine like to use pseudonyms and in some circumstances it guarantees anonymity. A CEO that is on both Twitter and Facebook, shares day-to-day insights of the daily working life of a CEO. His secrecy allows him to make more forthright remarks about business funding and development.

LinkedIn does not allow the use of pseudonyms, but most other systems are less concerned about them. Where ever possible be consistent in your username, use vanity names for your profile where they are available. Having named user accounts is always preferable. The author uses 'pgiblett' for the majority of his Social Media accounts. Make changes to your on-line profiles can be challenging. Making one site the master and permeating may be best in ensuring consistency. One of the problems here is that certain profiles can become out-of-date and forgotten. Try to reduce inconsistencies when making profile changes.

Pictures are an important part of a Social Media profile. This topic alone could fill several chapters, so we make this brief. You should always have a picture or avatar and the one you select should be reasonably professional. LinkedIn insists that the picture should be of you and not your dog or your grandchildren. Such a rule may go over the top, but your profile picture should be professional.

Brand images are appropriate on many sites. Facebook, Twitter and others do allow such images. Use of recognisable images will allow customers to associate themselves with your corporate intervention. Take a look at the other brands in your marketplace that are currently active and gain an idea of how they portray themselves.

Further Reading and References:

Dear Miss Social Media Manners... By Jennifer Laycock at

http://www.searchengineguide.com/jennifer-laycock/dear-miss-social-media-manners.php

Social Media Marketing - Mind Your Manners By Laura Lake at

http://marketing.about.com/b/2009/07/20/social-media-marketing-mind-your-manners.htm

Are Good Manners Out of Style? By Thomas M. Schmitz at:

http://www.trumpinitiative.com/blog/post/2009/09/are-good-manners-out-of-style.cfm

Good Manners and Social Marketing by Cynthia Nowicki at:

http://rithims.com/wordpress/2009/07/twelve-important-social-marketing-manners/

Section 3

Defining a Social Media Strategy

Defining Your Strategy

Whenever a business is faced with new realities it is essential to identify how adapt to the new challenges. This section discusses aspects which will impact and influence that strategy. Ultimately your strategy must be right for your business and must be deployable.

How to Leverage Social Media Channels for Business Success

This is perhaps one of the key concerns of CEOs or business owners. Leveraging the Social Media channel as a communication tool is of-course a priority. Yet this step requires a leap in thinking if executed successfully. There are many so-called 'Social Media Marketing experts' talking on this subject on a daily basis. The majority of these are advertising people who are simply advising businesses on how to leverage Social Media sites as a tool for traditional advertising.

Now, there is nothing wrong with leveraging the channel as an advertising mechanism, but it is only a tiny part in leveraging the Social Media Channel for business success. It is important to take a more holistic view. There are three pillars to leveraging Social Media for business success:

- Building a communication & collaborative capability
- Intelligent intervention in the marketplace
- Generating revenue as a trusted advisor

Some advertising specialists think only in terms of generating in income from this channel, but this approach will not ultimately lead to success. So lets look at each of these in turn

Communications & Collaboration

The whole history of business involves communication, in-fact trade or barter may have been one of the reasons we humans learned to talk. Humans are adaptive creatures and new communications capabilities will always be arriving, in fact it seems to be a large part behind driving many

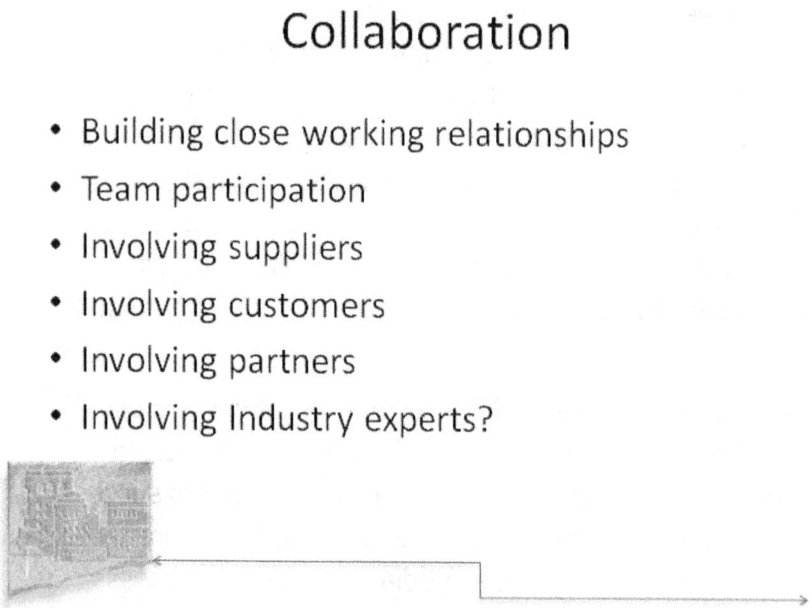
Collaboration
• Building close working relationships
• Team participation
• Involving suppliers
• Involving customers
• Involving partners
• Involving Industry experts?

technological advances. Today we face a changing world of business communications, everything is more rapid, in short bite sized chunks. We naturally want to be involved in a dialogue before we buy anything, the net result is that we want to trust those products that we purchase.

From a business standpoint part of that dialogue involves a wide range of people who are involved in getting any product to market. This more than ever before is a collaborative process. In the past collaboration has been about reaching out via email, we often forget to involve all the knowledge-holders within an organisation, let alone with suppliers, customers etc. Collaborative efforts have always been based on team membership.

The collaborative challenge today is to involve a wider audience, including suppliers, customers, and other partners we are able to improve the level of communication and take appropriate action. Understanding that a customer's business is closing early on Wednesday for a corporate event and keeping the trucking partner in the loop will ensure that deliveries are re-scheduled and arrive at an appropriate time for processing. Included are Industry Experts; don't know the answer to a problem – look it up on-line or find an expert. Social media is bringing those experts closer to your business as a normal resource.

The section "Invest On Relationships" discusses the value to be gained from improving collaboration within the workplace. Everyone has competencies they bring with them from either their social life or prior workplace. They have a sphere of collaboration, starting with themselves, expanding to the people they work with. This builds through teams and departments to the company as a whole. Each step potentially adds expertise. Ultimately it is the individual spheres of influence touch customers, suppliers, and third party partners with whom we are able to build a trusting relationship over time.

Intelligent Intervention

When people are talking about your brand your finger needs to be right on the pulse! The response needs to be immediate, proportionate and relevant.

Remember that Googling your brand or company should show your web-site to the top of the search results, but it is

Image Management

- What is being said about
  - my organisation?
  - my brand/product?
  - my competitors?
- Piracy? Legal?
- Developing a Social Media Intelligence
- Rewarding any recommendations
- Help people with problems

unlikely to show what someone just said about you on Twitter. Using traditional search engines it takes time and a lot of effort to discover what was said yesterday. A negative blog may take months to discover via traditional search.

A person who starts a hate campaign against your product or company needs to be placated before the press come knocking on the door.

Social Media Intelligence is about knowing what is being said about a product and having a plan to respond proportionately in any given situation. The triggers are questions about 'What is being said about my organisation, my product, my competitors?' To a large extent these are traditional market research questions, but we have never before had such a powerful view about people's thinking. People are giving their views every day about topics relevant to your business. It is driven by what is important to people at a specific point in time.

In addition we can link this general knowledge with a knowledge of the views of customers, when retaining social media ID's of customers when they make on-line comments (and remember there may be many). This information is closely allied to marketing intelligence.

Monitoring solutions are available that will automatically monitor the Internet buzz and throw up an alert when action is needed. Rewarding recommendations is a key. What do you do when an independent person spontaneously says something good about your product and company? At the very least it is important to thank them, one airline thanked a customer by giving a 25% discount on flights because of something said on Twitter.

Helping people with their problems is one of the best ways of intervening in the marketplace. Solving someone else's problem will win you kudos, even if the person does not use your product. What happens next time they are looking to buy? You will be high on their wish list and possibly the only candidate.

Revenue Opportunity

Advertising on the Social Media channel will bring an income, but this will generally be at the same rate as advertising on the Internet. We may be able to tweak this a few points by focusing the advertising for specific demographic groups. At the end of the day the Social Media channel is based in trust and expertise. This is where leveraging this channel requires

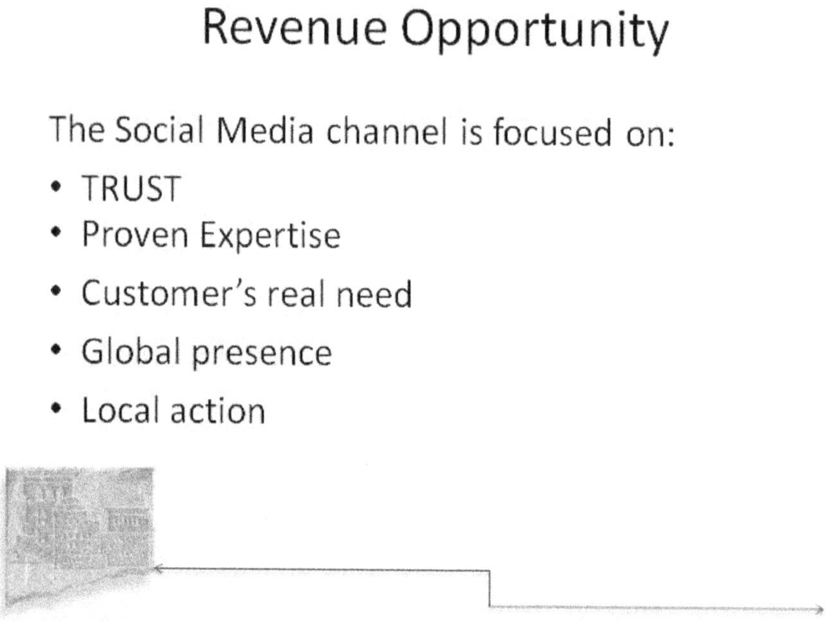
Revenue Opportunity
The Social Media channel is focused on:
• TRUST
• Proven Expertise
• Customer's real need
• Global presence
• Local action

a shift in thinking. The marketing communication budget is not simply about advertising, it must now think about involvement. A corporation's ability to leverage the Social Media channel to collaborate and be involved in the marketplace becomes important. It builds a revenue based on trust and expertise in specific areas.

A prospective customer who has found you through a specific Social Media is interested in the services that you have to offer, they will come to you because they already trust you and they are interested in your product. Hey isn't this better than Yellow Pages?

The ROI of Social Media

Social Media can be viewed by many as the current must-have, but at what cost? Are corporations setting aside the ROI in order to jump start their enterprise social media presence?

It has been said that it is not possible to identify an ROI for collaborative improvements and that we only see the real improvements in the rear-view mirror. Yet defining an ROI for any project or proposed solution is about producing a best estimate at the time the need is perceived. That is as relevant for any Social Media implementation as it is for any other corporate change. Remember the major impact of social medial is more in the area of business than with the technology that underpins it.

The other aspect here is about contributing to an improvement in business results. This should be measurable through Business Intelligence. It is valid to measure the contribution made by Social Media to the bottom line. This must include a value for the collaborative effort, and for web intervention (including the real value from promotions offered). Spending should be appropriate, but will always be based on business drivers.

Where do We Find Customers, or Prospects?

Determining a strategy based on this question will largely depend on what your marketplace is, who your typical customers are, their demographic characteristics and their psyche. The person making the marketing investment decisions will tend to turn towards sites that satisfy their own comfort zone when developing a Social Media strategy, which may not always be the smartest move. For example using Social Media when trying to promote a new product aimed at on-line teens; you will not find many teens on LinkedIn for example as the site is focused towards professionals and executives and the site policy states that it is for people over 18; yet this may be where the executive spends their on-line life.

In order to market to people through Social Media it is necessary more than ever before to develop a brand persona and bring that persona to life, more so than for any other form of communication. This has characteristics recognised by target market – they will identify with it. The prospective customer needs to feel that they are communicating directly with that 'person', so it is necessary to breath life into the product.

Generally social media activity is via the brand. A corporation having several brands focused on different market needs must think about the needs of each brand within a separate strategy. Continuing on the theme of the teen market you will need to understand the different locations for teens interested in music than for teens interested in sporting goods, although there may be some crossover obviously. For the business seeking to intervene in social media it is important they find the right site to be involved in from the literally hundreds available. This choice will almost certainly include the style of music, since each tends to have very different sub-cultures.

This involves a lot of research into the right locations to use for the relevant market. It is also seen to be relevant to the prospects out there – having someone aged 50 writing the posts for a teen site might not be a smart move. Would they know whether it is cool, kool, kewl, or hot? The latest recruit or even the latest teen idol you are trying to generate interest in may be the right person to make the posts – spelling mistakes and all.

Closer to the Customer - Do we Understand their Needs?

Getting closer to the customer has been an ever present business challenge over much of the last quarter of a century. The average corporation has mountains of customer performance data, yet most corporations still believe they do not understand their customer. Customer Relationship Management has become a modern oxymoron and it seems that the more that we know the more we still need to know.

The average corporation possesses a slew of systems, the majority relating to customer activities like orders, billing, production, supply chain, all of these are integrated to some extent to the CRM. New technologies appear yet there is continued talk about improving the customer experience has been a constant theme over the last quarter century.

As Social Media is added to the corporate arsenal "Improving customer communications" is quoted as one of the key reasons for adoption. Do not misunderstand: each layer is essential in getting to know how the customer acts. With

Social Media it is possible that we may start to understand some of the driving forces behind their actions. To some extent we have been categorising customers in order to pattern match them, which in turn allows the business to focus better on what it perceives their needs are, then along comes a tool that allows customers to talk directly to the corporation on a one-to-one basis. Each business should be holding multiple one-to-one conversations simultaneously, each may be different, yet each gives an insight into that customer. Each can point to different services provided that are good and bad. Perhaps at last it is possible to garner some real intelligence about the mindset of the customer.

Yet Social Media is a promotional tool isn't it? Actually Social Media is not a tool for any specific area of the business. It certainly impacts corporate marketing communication, but it is also a part of customer service efforts. It also contributes to product development. etc. etc. etc. The key here is that the customer is now talking each and every area of the corporation. Are you paying attention? Do you have a strategy to respond?

The frustrated customer has always been one to make a lot of noise. Arguably there is too much time spent thinking about them. Yet in the modern communication rich world it is important we listen and respond appropriately. Everything is done so publicly today and it is important that the response is proportionate and focused. Everyone probably has a relative or friend who is frustrated with the service a particular business offers and makes it their mission to tell everyone they know not to shop there. Well with Social Media they can publish their "Top 10 reasons not to eat at McDonalds" on a blog and leverage SEO expertise to have it appear on search engines above, or very near, the company's main website. Not only will it shout their complaints, it will do so while they are asleep and with the right amount of Social Media noise (especially if this activity goes unanswered) they may be able to influence a significant percent of the population.

It is therefore vital that the business tracks what is being said about them and their products or brands on this very public forum and respond appropriately. More than ever before the response made must to be honest. It is better to remain silent that tell a lie. It is also better to admit that your product has a fault than to deploy a advertising message as a cover up. Customers prefer to hear "we goofed" than "you are misinterpreting how this product should be used". Things do go wrong from time to time. To err is human, we all know that, but businesses also make mistakes. Organisations sometimes have to admit a mistake and bringing clients or the general public to that point can need prickly crisis management. In the Social Media world you can gain respect by admitting mistakes, but it is important to be sincere.

The response given is perhaps the most important thing to be managed when a customer is complaining in such a public forum. Yet who should give the response? Marketing? Customer Services? Product Development? It is probably best that the response sound personal and genuine (heart felt). No response should ever sound like it came from any particular department. Who responds depends on the circumstances, and may even be the CEO if the complaint warrants it.

A More Holistic Approach to Marketing Communication

Mark Landiak tells us that Customer Services is not a department, and the same applies to Marketing is not a department in a corporation. Landiak talks of marketing being a verb; an **action** word and as such it is an action that needs to be performed across the whole business.

Throughout this discussion about Social Media it has become clear that the marketing aspect is about generating a more holistic message that runs through everything that the corporation does. There is a tendency to think that all outgoing messages need to be cleared by the head of Corporate Communications or by the company lawyer. Yet accounting people talk to customers daily, as do delivery people, and production staff. They need to as an ongoing part of their job, yet these conversations do not need clearing. All of these contribute to the overall customer experience. They are, if you like part of the overall communication, eventhough there is no sales activity involved.

Holistic thinking is that every person employed by the business whether this is the CEO, the salesman, the receptionist, or the accounts clerk are all spokespeople for the company in some little way. What matters is that the whole organisation is adhering to a set of goals, not every individual message sent. Each person in every activity in the business is focused to some extent on building awareness for the company, its brands, and products. How we manage the relationship with a prospect or a customer needs to be defined across the organisation. Internally staff know what is expected of them in performing their role. Yet every person in the business can continue to work as they have but additionally have a brand-building mindset in how they manage their part of the customer relationship.

Being mindful of this approach when thinking about who should be involved in the corporate Social Media deployment. It is clear that Social Media associates itself with trust based marketing. How better to demonstrate trustworthiness as a supplier than by demonstrating that you take an holistic and caring approach to managing your customer relationships. Who should answer the question "Why is my order late?" not Marketing, but Order Fulfilment.

Researching this aspect of Social Media deployment we sought authorities to support this approach from authoritative authors and was encouraged to know that there is support, particularly with writers like Jay Conrad Levinson talking about the "Guerrilla Marketing Mindset". The solution is not solely one for Social Media but relates to holistic business development. In Social Media we simply are adding to the traditional media tactics, the brochures, signs, and adverts. Levinson talks about a marketing mindset being "the way you think about how all of these activities and other things work together to achieve your marketing goals. It is about tying all your activity to the mission statement... understanding your target market, who will buy from you and why". (From *Guerrilla Marketing in 30 Days*).

It is clear he is talking about building relationships with customers and prospects – something that Social Media adds another dimension to in the corporate world. The why a person goes to their auto mechanic may be because they found them in Yellow pages, the why reason they go back is because they did a good job and kept within the allotted budget. The new dimension is that when someone asks you on Facebook to recommend an auto mechanic in your area then it is possible to make a recommendation based on work performed. This works for any size of organisation the global organisation can think globally, yet act locally. From the corporate standpoint it is always appropriate to thank a person for making a recommendation of your services, and the beauty of it is that this need not cost money – a simple, yet public, "*Thank You*" is often great currency.

Levinson says "Your marketing can be compared to breathing. You can't live very long on just a single breath. It takes many breaths, one right after another. Marketing works the same way. You won't attract new customers or new business with one marketing initiative. You keep breathing to stay alive. You continue marketing to make more trips to the bank."

Deployment:

It is a Business Decision to Make

A couple of thoughts:

> "Research has shown that in most organisations it is a small number of people are responsible for a large amount of web usage. Adding [Social Media] applications into the mix does allow more opportunity

> for overburdening the corporate network. It is this more than anything that concerns the average corporation."

and:

> "The Internet is evolving [and] the corporation must understand the business benefit each technology bring and decide whether access to them is appropriate within their organisation, department, or work-group. Any technology will only bring real benefit when it is intuitive, easy to use, and has a clearly stated value proposition."

Over the past couple of years social media drivers have become stronger for the corporation, yet according to the authors research corporate understanding has advanced very little. Every business has to think through the implications of the new media and how best to approach it. Revenue opportunities do not come about simply because the business leverages social media for advertising, they come about because of involvement in the media and because of interaction with people there.

Social media provides another level of communication. To leverage the media correctly we are investing in relationships. In fact it can be argued that the media is primarily a collaboration tool. Involvement is about strengthening the relationships that we are involved in. People involved in collaboration have distinct expertise and specialities and each can help others complete their job. This process happens with or without social media. Social media is simply providing tools that can make this collaboration happen at the speed of the web. Here we are simply managing relationships with smarter tools. A return on investment can be measured simply by looking at smarter communications alone.

Ultimately an individuals sphere of influence touch customers and suppliers, they may also touch various third party partners with whom we are able to build a trusting relationship over time.

In this respect it is interesting to keeping an open eye on new technologies like Google Wave. This should be a further collaborative tool in the corporate communications arsenal. Within 5 years email as structured today will have changed forever if Wave is successful.

In 2008 it was proposed that "There is between a 2 and 6 fold productivity enhancement for any given large organization to adopt collaborative technologies. It can also be argued that early adoption will be progressive and lead to a corporation being at the forefront of an industry". This is still true today, the Social Media market is still immature, but right now knowledge is building and perhaps productivity levels can be even higher when deployed correctly.

Yet also recently many managers have been asking "Have we missed the Web 2.0 bandwagon?" Clearly this executive was concerned that having not been an early adopter they were now too late to take advantage of Social Media capabilities.

The concept of being "too late" is an interesting one, given credence by Bill Gates in his book "The Road Ahead" published in 1995, where he stated many that a business must be on the web by the year 2000 in order to survive. Yet today many businesses are only on the web because of those words, their sites being totally ineffective as a sales or advertising tool. Actually it is not essential for every business to be on the web, let alone use social media. The auto-repair business at the end of the street probably derives little benefit from having a web-site, after all you cannot book your car in for a service through their site, let alone get a progress check as it goes through each stage. Any business can elect to get involved with a specific technology at any stage in its development. The decision relating to deployment should be backed up with an identifiable return on investment and a consideration of the process impact it brings with it.

One important policy decision that still has to be made is "**What tools should we be using?**" and "**Who should use Social Media?**". These decisions are business decisions, not technological ones.

Further Reading and References:

_"The Advantage of Good Business Intelligence" By Peter B. Giblett at:

http://cio-perspectives.com/2009/02/the-advantage-of-good-business-intelligence/

"Making mistakes: Admit your errors" by Wayne Hurlbert found at:

http://blogbusinessworld.blogspot.com/2007/01/making-mistakes-admit-your-errors.html

"What should managers do when things go wrong?" By Robert Heller is found at:

http://www.fastcompany.com/blog/robert-heller/business-management/what-should-managers-do-when-things-go-wrong

"How to Make a Graceful Retreat" by Maged Sedky at:

http://www.bcbusinessonline.ca/bcb/business-sense/need-know/-office/2009/11/04/how-make-graceful-retreat

"Gaining Respect By Admitting Mistakes" by Phil Holberton

http://www.holberton.com/newsletter3.html

Crisis Management method by Value Based Management at:

http://www.valuebasedmanagement.net/methods_crisis_management_advice.html

"What Customers Expect From You Today" by Mark Landiak

http://ezinearticles.com/?What-Customers-Expect-From-You-Today&id=853236

Jay Conrad Levinson about the Marketing Mindset:

Web: http://www.gmarketing.com/

Print: Guerrilla Marketing in 30 Days

"Realizing Value from Social Networks: A Life Cycle Model" by The Global Human Capital Journal

"Social media can strengthen customer relationships" by Thor Harris found at:

http://www.icis.com/Articles/2009/10/19/9255330/social-media-can-strengthen-customer-relationships.html

"Feeling the Fear" by Elizabeth Bennet at:

http://www.cioinsight.com/c/a/Trends/Feeling-the-Fear-but-Doing-It-Anyway-324289/

Tension in Collaboration by Bruce Lewin at:

http://www.fourgroups.com/blog/archives/24/the-tension-in-collaboration/

Section 4

How do my Connections Assist in Building my Business?

Building a Communication & Collaborative Capability

From the dawn of human history we have communicated with each other. The requirement to trade and barter is perhaps one of the original primitive desires that drove humans to improve their ability to communicate, to improve the number of words used etc. Speech is undoubtedly the first means of sentient communication. As a species we have gone on to greater heights from there, and possibly business has been at the heart of it all.

Constantly humans find more ways to communicate and collaborate. Social Media is one of many answers, albeit an important one in the changing world of business communications.

The Changing World of Business Communications

There are several types of communication that are important to the average business today:

- ◊ Direct one-to-one, a dialogue
- ◊ One-to-many, broadcasting
- ◊ Many-to-many, such as in a meeting

On a "**One to One**" basis we communicate directly or through another medium. There are differences in how we communicate but there is generally a dialogue that occurs in any conversation. The approach may be different say for a letter (if anyone writes these anymore ☺) or an email than in a conversation, but it is a dialogue nonetheless. In a conversation tend to will deal with one point at a time, whereas in a letter we tend to include all of the related detail before sending it.

Email differs from a normal letter in that it is not purely a one-to-one messaging tool, it allows us to send that same message to multiple people at the same time and with the use of BCC (blind carbon copy) send it to a person that no one else knows is privy to the information. We developed the ability to broadcast early in human history as well – remember the smoke-signals used by Native Americans were almost certainly used in other ancient societies; even 16 century England had a fire warning system used to send messages rapidly across the country in order to prepare for an expected attack of the Spanish Armada, allowing them to muster forces at a time when sending a message by traditional means was agonisingly slow.

"**One to Many**" messages are used in a multitude of ways, like a newspaper article, telegraph, radio, television. The 'presenter' makes their statement via the appropriate media. Today we are putting a lot of this information on-line in the form of websites or blogs. The majority of information still follows the process of one person posting for a group of others (large or small) to see.

"**Many to Many**" communications don't really exist through any of the traditional communications media. A meeting may give an opportunity for everyone to speak, but it is in reality held through a series on one to many communications. Generally humans are not able to handle multiple simultaneous conversations at the same time; so we have developed a set of unspoken rules, conventions, or protocols, that enables us to achieve the effect of a many-to-many conversation.

Computers on the other hand are able do multiple things at the same time more effectively and they can communicate with other computers at a speed that allows messages to cross the globe in an instant.

The changing world of business communications is largely about empowering collaboration between people who are interested in a particular outcome. In business relationships have always been vital for success, in fact it plays on another basic part of the human nature. The need for a team to work together for the success of the voyage is as vital for the crew of a trawler facing a ferocious storm as it is for your business.

Each person involved brings with them something unique that helps their team succeed. Today we are able to contribute in so many ways and continue adding value to business processes. With the use of Social Media it is even possible to have customers make a contribution to product development which can be a vital part of a business's success story. It is important to remember that collaboration is a very personal thing. Each and every person has a sphere of collaboration, which is about them, their team, the department they work for, the company, customers, suppliers, third-parties, industry experts, etc. Even their friends perhaps have a role to play.

Ultimately the changing world of business communications is about improving business's ability to collaborate. It is about bringing the right people together, cost effectively, to solve a specific problem, then moving on.

A Short History of Communications

From the dawn of humanity we have constantly enhanced our ability to communicate. Humans as a species have invented new words, new languages and new ways to tell each other things, particularly as we excerpted more control over the environment around us. Here are a few facts about communications over the short history of mankind:

Homo Sapiens learned to **speak** (somewhere between 40,000 and 100,000 years ago depending on the time-line believed for the birth of the species). What is certain is that we spoke very early in human development. Basic words like 'yes' and 'no' were the first human inventions. We learned to **write**. Now no-one is certain of when the first writing was done. Early symbols were thought to have been developed about 30,000 years ago. What is certain is that written records were developed independently in four different civilizations across the world, namely Mesopotamia, China, Egypt, and Mesoamerica between 6,000 and 10,000 years ago. These are the pre-cursor's to modern writing.

Mankind has had other forms of communications, like smoke signals. Undoubtedly **written messages** were sent to one another as soon as we could use a portable medium, huge stones with Egyptian writing on them could hardly have been sent across the country. The Chinese are known to have written on bamboo at about the same time that papyrus was used in Egypt and Mesopotamia.

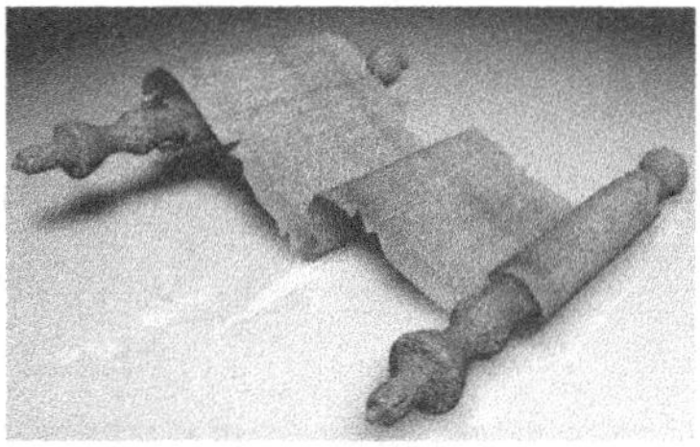

Papyrus was first used just before 2400 BC. **Scrolls** were made at this time by weaving papyrus sheets together so it is safe to assume that the first hand-written 'books' were produced at that time. The Chinese also made bamboo books at about this time. The first accounting ledgers may also date from this time.

Paper was thought to have been invented in the first or second century AD in China and was widely available in Europe by the 12th century. The modern **printing press** was invented in 1440 (However wood block printing was available about 2000 years ago). There were also a series of associated discoveries like movable type, lithography, and others that improved printing methods. The first modern **newspaper** was in 1605 (however official bulletins existed in the Roman era carved on metal or stone to be posted in public places).

In the UK the **post office** improved the efficiency of message delivery and in 1842 making all letters a standard pre-paid cost. The **stamp** was invented.

It is at this point that your story of communications tales a twist as we looked at other ways to communicate more rapidly, particularly over long distances like the vast tracts of America and as colonial powers in Europe built their colonies across the globe. These are the foundations of electronic communications age.

The invention the **telegraph** in the 1830's gave the ability for rapid long distance communication, via wire. Messages had to be coded (through Morse code) in order to be sent across the wires but required a skilled operator to both send and receive messages. The **telephone** invented in 1875 by comparison was much more civilised than the telegraph. It brought services closer to the consumer with limited intervention by skilled technicians. By 1880 the first telephone directory was printed. Obviously the first telephone is a far cry from the modern system.

Radio, or **wireless** communications were invented in either 1891 or 1895 according to opposing claims. This brought about the ability for the first time to send messages to a mass audience. The modern and popular invention of **television** added pictures to the voice of radio in 1926.

Radio telephony was first used on the first-class passenger trains between Berlin and Hamburg in 1926. This was the precursor to the modern **mobile** (or **cell**ular) **phone**. They have been gaining popularity since the 1950's when the first mobile devices were introduced, but the 80's and 90's were the era of real expansion.

Each of these devices 'democratised' the sending of messages by electronic means. The original telephone and telegraph may not have originally used electricity as such but their technologies ultimately facilitated electronic communications and making the next set of communications capabilities possible. The following machines represent the heart of business communications for much of the 20th century.

The **Facsimile Machine** was invented as early as 1843 but it went through a number of reinventions till 1902 when it was possible to send messages between two machines. The 'Bildtelegraph' (or picture telegraph) was used in Europe, notably for the transmission of a wanted-person photograph from Paris to London in 1908. Although it was not in popular use till the 1970's and despite the popularity of email today refuses to die.

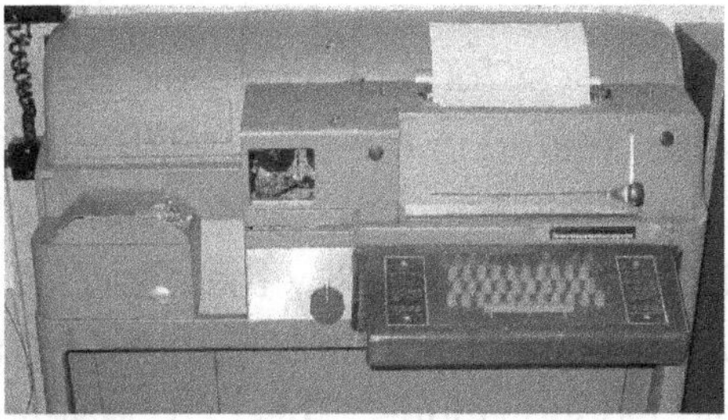

A global teleprinter network, called the **Telex** network, was established in the 1920s, and was used through most of the 20th century for business communications.

The Internet was arguably created in 1969 when the first ARPANET (Advanced Research Projects Agency Network) link was established between the University of California, Los Angeles and the Stanford Research Institute. Soon after many world universities had their computers linked together via the Joint academic network – JANET. These precursors transitioned, through work performed by the US Department of Defense, into what we know today as the Internet through the course of the 1970's and 80's. Any former United States Vice President who tells you they invented the Internet is wrong. This has in turn facilitated a whole raft of new communications opportunities for us. Each building of the foundation of the idea of inter-computer links.

In 1971 the first **email** application was created on ARPANET. Early programs had limited functions and were command line driven, but established the basic communications model (including the 'name@host' notation) that still exists today – an email gets sent to someone's mailbox, where it can be picked up at a later time.

Instant Messaging, or on-line chat also appeared around this time. Two people were able to talk MSN style, but they were limited to 80 characters and only one person could type at a time.

The earliest form of electronic **Bulletin Boards**, or BBS, were created in the early 1970's with a notion called Community Memory, in 1972, in the Berkeley area in California. However by the mid 70's people realised that it was possible to bring together on-line communities of like minded individuals. This can be seen as one of the pre-cursor's to modern Social Media (except not in real time). It was possible to dial-up to ask a question, but getting answers could take several weeks. Limited on-line chat was also possible. Internet forums replaced the traditional BBS in the 90's with ability for instant access and instant responses.

The creation of the first We**b Log** (or **Blog**) is more difficult to ascertain. By the millennium it is certain that there were a number of on-line magazines or journals in existence. Writer Jim Howard claims 1982 as the date of the first blog others define on-line lists of links as 1994, diary as 1995, and news postings as 1997 (CNet News has a brief discussion on this topic at http://news.cnet.com/2100-1025_3-6168681.html).

Wikipedia, the world first **online encyclopaedia** was formally launched in 2001. This became the dawn of a new era of collaborative publishing. Today Wikipedia includes several million freely usable articles and pages in over one hundred languages worldwide, and content from millions of contributors. What is important here is that specialist wiki's have a variety of uses across the world that can include the rules of a particular sport to corporate business processes.

These have been amazing advances and every success breeds another advance in our ability to communicate. We see email as instant today, yet when it was created it was perhaps less reliable than the postal network at delivering messages. A person had to know they had an email waiting, often necessitating a phone call to tell them. How far we have now gone with the email arriving on the person's mobile phone almost the moment it is sent.

The first recognizable **Social Media** site, Six Degrees, was launched in 1997. Unfortunately it closed in 2000 as people were not yet ready to bear their soul to the world. Although Social Media would come into its own after 2003 with sites like MySpace, LinkedIn launching. Other sites launched over the next few months. Bebo, Facebook, YouTube and others launched in 2005 (although Facebook had private users some months before this).

The concept of six degrees of separation popularised by John Guare. The idea that, if a person is one step away from each person they know and two steps away from each person who is known by one of the people they know, then everyone is at most six steps away from any other person on the planet. It is a profound thought... how every person can become a new door, providing an opening for other people into new worlds. This author remains unconvinced of this theory, but it is granted that Social Media certainly seems to be bringing people closer together.

Communications Tools
Isn't what we have today already enough?

The point of this short history of communication is to show that humans seem to have an almost infinite desire to communicate more effectively. We are inherently social animals. We learned to talk because we are essentially social animals and we have moved this ability to higher and higher levels ever since.

Few of these communications inventions have become extinct simply because of new inventions. The **Telegram** and the **Telex** are perhaps the most notable exceptions here. We have simply adopted the new technology as being able to help us do things differently (perhaps even more efficiently). The use of the postal service has declined since the popular use of email and instant messaging in the mid to late 90's. But post is still essential in delivering bills, magazines and parcels.

The point is humans are adaptive and new communications capabilities will always be arriving. take for example the recent launch of Google Wave in 2009 which brings new collaborative capabilities. Wave is compared most to email, but in fact it is more like a combination of email, instant Messaging and Social Media within one tool. Does this herald the end of the road for email? Perhaps it does, and perhaps not. The point is that we will inevitably adopt new mechanisms to improve how we collaborate between groups that need to work together. We are simply adding a new layer that can advance capabilities even further.

The future ultimately is a blank page to steal a writer's analogy. It is what we do with it that matters.

Relationships Matter

In the last section concluded that humans are adaptive creatures and new communications capabilities will always be arriving. This was of course discussing the technological features of communications. It the end of the day we would have not invented this array of communications technologies over the years had relationships not mattered to humans.

Relationships do matter, which is why we keep seeking improvements in how we stay in contact with each other, right back to the times of the caveman communication would not happen without relationships and relationships would not happen without communication. This is somewhat a circular reference, but it is undoubtedly true. Communications and relationships are key to the development of humanity.

In "Lucy: The Beginnings of Humankind" Donald Johanson and Maitland Edey postulate a theory about the development of humankind and the enlargement of human brains and the development of language to a complex set of interrelated triggers that enabled man to stand erect, communicate, develop an affinity with tools. There are, of course, many competing theories about human development but it is doubtful that human kind would be on this planet today but for its ability to handle complex problems and to convey solutions to each other effectively.

This is not intended to be a discussion in the area of paleoanthropology, although the workings of ancient man can sometimes teach us much about who we are. The only reason for touching on the subject is in further understanding communications and relationship building. We know that almost as soon as we became human we were able to communicate verbally. Basic words like 'yes', 'no', and 'hungry' were probably the first human inventions (even before fire), we have simply been developing from there. The fact that that written records were developed independently in four different civilizations across the world thousands of years ago shows that simple speech was never enough for our species.

A basic part of human development is also about working together, co-operatively in teams. One of the images this writer recalls from his youth was a teacher telling the class about ancient man hunting and killing woolly mammoths. Given these creatures were larger than elephants and more ferocious hunting was definitely done by teamwork. So the cartoon of one caveman clubbing another is good for jest, but probably has no basis in reality. Humans have always been social creatures that understand working together for the common good.

It is well known that fire was one of humankind's first tools. It would not be surprising to find that most ancient cultures developed an ability to communicate with each other by smoke signals very soon after understanding how to manage fire. The ancient telegraph? It may have assisted tribal unity while the hunting parties were away from the home area. Writing probably came when we had more complex messages to convey. Papyrus and paper certainly came about as humans became more refined in our culture.

Most of other communications requirements seem to stem from this point as we moved from person to person communications to the need to broadcast a message to all. That is the thinking behind the printing press, books, newspapers, radio, television, internet, blogs and other mass broadcast techniques. If you think about that concept it requires a leap of faith that we will have an audience out there who are waiting to hear what we have to say. Yet as that saying goes "if you build it they will come".

So we humans like to talk and be talked to.

Clearly mass broadcast only satisfies a small element of human desires. We also needed to improvements to interpersonal communications hence the letter, telegraph, telephone, email, instant message and other forms of personal communications, including Social Media. We had a form of Twitter hundreds if not thousands of years ago – think back to your youth for a minute and the postcard notices in the window of the newsagent, tobacconist, or supermarket. According to some historians such message boards were also used in Roman times to communicate between citizens, so we have posted private messages in a public place a long time ago.

Collaboration is one aspect where modern social media is taking communications to a whole new level. Yet it must be remembered this is not our first opportunity to collaborate, remember ancient man and their ability to act collaboratively to topple the mammoth, part of man's ability to start controlling the environment in which we live. The ability to work collaboratively is increasingly important. We can be sure that Wikipedia will not be the last collaborative publication.

The importance of relationship building within the business world is also clear to be seen. Whether a mail room clerk or a CEO relationships are paramount. They take on extra importance when relationships add value to the organisation. It has often been said that people prefer to work with people they like – in fact, rightly or wrongly, it is often the basis for hiring another person. But it does not end there every person in every role has to build relationships with others to be successful at their job:

- ◊ The salesman with the prospect or customer
- ◊ The buyer with the supplier
- ◊ The shipper with the logistics companies in the supply chain.

These are the most obvious, but the list goes on across the whole of the business. Relationships matter doubly when working together in teams, e.g. the project team implementing the new accounting system. Few, if any, jobs in the modern corporation are performed in isolation.

Communications are of course at the heart of Social Media. When leveraged correctly Social Media is a tool for building relationships with new prospects. In fact it should be one of the entry points for future connections. These connections may start as mere names in an electronic form if we do not do something with them to turn them into real relationships. Not every relationship will add direct value to the business, yet they may still think about you in their next conversation and that may be the route to your next customer. That is why it is important to build a relationship of trust.

The whole history of communications is about adding new capabilities. Relationships do matter in building everything we do in business today. There is a clear value to be gained from improving collaboration within the workplace. Organisational Development experts have been encouraging corporations to be more collaborative during much of the past 30 years, and possibly longer. We have all made great steps to improve teamwork particularly for those who work in a project environment, yet teamwork is only a small part of the collaborative environment which is possible today.

Adding Social Media into the mix adds a whole new dimension, even if you just involve people within the workplace. We work with some amazing people and you never know what knowledge they possess. That knowledge when applied to a problem can take the organisation forward in leaps and bounds.

Sections entitled "Invest on Relationships" and "Don't Set Aside the ROI in Building your Social Media Solution" below

both discuss the importance of building relationships and collaboration within the new and evolving Social Media.

Take each individual we can look at their collaborative sphere of influence. Starting with themselves, they can expand their influence by working with another person. Do a good job and their reputation grows. It can be further enhanced through teams, their department to the company as a whole. There should be nothing new about this principle, but it is the foundation for doing business in the social media world. Each step of this process brings additional expertise to assist in defining a solution. Ultimately spheres of influence touch customers and suppliers, they may also touch various third party partners like haulage companies. This is ultimately about building and enhancing relationships, that in themselves add value to the business.

Collaboration

Consider the following:

- Building close working relationships
- Team participation
- Involving suppliers
- Involving customers
- Involving partners
- Involving Industry experts?

Up-to now collaboration tended to have been about reaching out via telephone or email, we often forget to involve all the knowledge-holders within an organisation, let alone with suppliers, customers and others. Involving them it is possible to improve the level of communication and take appropriate action. Understanding that a customer's business is closing early on Wednesday for a corporate event and keeping the trucking partner in the loop will ensure that deliveries are re-scheduled. They must be viewed as an extended member of the team.

Industry experts as a category bring in knowledge to enhance business capabilities. Don't know the answer to a problem – look it up on-line or find an expert. Social media is bringing those experts closer to us as a natural resource.

Invest On Relationships

The last section discussed the importance of building relationships and collaboration within the new and evolving Social Media. Recently The Global Human Capital Journal (GHCJ) published "Realizing Value from Social Networks: A Life Cycle Model", which certainly contained some interesting points, none the least of which was the sub-heading "IOR Before ROI"

Obviously IOR (invest on relationships) is a play on words being the reverse of ROI and in reality, with the use of proper English, it should read "Invest In Relationships", yet keeping with the theme here allows poetic justice.

There is a clear value to be gained from improving collaboration within the workplace. Organisational Development experts have been encouraging corporations to be more collaborative during much of the past 30 years, and possibly longer. We have all made great steps to improve teamwork particularly for those who work in a project environment, yet teamwork is only a small part of the collaborative environment which is possible today. Adding Social Media into the mix adds a whole new dimension, even if you just involve people within the workplace. We work with some amazing people and you never know what knowledge they possess. That knowledge when applied to a problem can take the organisation forward in leaps and bounds.

It is possibly easier for a person who has spent his entire life in a project environment to say this than it is for parts of the organisation that seem purely operational. Yet everyone has competencies they bring with them from their social life or prior workplace. The Global Human Capital Journal is right in saying that "Firms need to define their USPs and be honest: how many clients map closely to the USP?" and "How long does it take to find and develop a prospect with a unique buying need (UBN) that corresponds?" Of course every business is looking to make money. The basic proposition about Social Media is that every individual needs, as a first step, to expand their collaborative sphere. Expertise is vital to the success of this process.

Each of the elements of this value sphere bring in distinct expertise and specialities and each helps one individual complete their job. This process happens with or without Social Media. Social Media is simply providing tools that can make this collaboration happen at the speed of the web.

Obviously this example provides a simplified corporate structure, but at the end of the day the model still holds true for a large multi-national corporation, there are simply more layers within the sphere of influence, yet we are still investing in relationships.

Managing Social Media Relationships

Traditionally we have built all of our relationships face-to-face or through the telephone. With the advent of Social Media we have started to make connections that we would not otherwise make. In making such a connection we also can start to know people without having many of the traditional contact points, their address, their telephone, their email address. To some people this can present a challenge, others feel a certain cushion of safety by not giving out real world information.

Yet at some point the relationship must move from a virtual relationship to a real-world one in order to transact business. Largely how this happens will depend on the medium, but it must be based on the connection having been made.

LinkedIn members get access to their first level connections' address card, which can be downloaded into Outlook. But with Facebook and other networks there is no access to the contact data for your direct connections. So social media relationships do need to be turned into real relationships in order for them to relevant for business building. Attaching a real customer's Twitter address to the contact information held ties that information neatly together.

The challenge can be to take a virtual prospect that that is interested in your brand in the social media world and turn that into a real-world contact. The key is to take the relationship out of the social media realm and into the real world. Get their contact points – email at a minimum; and start a private one-to-one dialogue. This dialogue will be founded on the things in the public domain but will be driven by a desire to set the relationship on a more solid business foundation. Here there will be significant differences according to the type of business that you are conducting. Where you business connects directly with the public (e.g. a supermarket) then the on-line personas may always remain distinct from the person visiting the store.

Where a business is providing products or services to other businesses then any desire to ultimately execute some form of business relationship must be solidified into the real world. Here social media simply provided the connection mechanism it is how the human relationship is built that is crucial to growing business.

Further Reading and Related Articles:

For information about ARPANET see the associate Wikipedia entry at http://en.wikipedia.org/wiki/ARPANET

Blogs turn 10--who's the father? By Declan McCullagh and Anne Broache is found at:

http://news.cnet.com/2100-1025_3-6168681.html

Who invented the Blog? By Jim Howard is published at:

http://www.showmeblog.com/home/2006/01/who_invented_th.html

History of Wikipedia is found at:

http://en.wikipedia.org/wiki/History_of_Wikipedia

Google Wave can be found at: http://wave.google.com/

"Lucy: The Beginnings of Humankind" Donald Johanson and Maitland Edey is available at:

http://www.amazon.com/Lucy-Beginnings-Humankind-Donald-Johanson/dp/0671724991/ref=sr_1_1?ie=UTF8&s=books&qid=1254776689&sr=8-1

The Global Human Capital Journal (GHCJ) published "Realizing Value from Social Networks: A Life Cycle Model" at

http://globalhumancapital.org/?p=696

Notes on Six Degrees of Separation by John Guare can be found at:

http://www.enotes.com/six-degrees

Section 5

Developing an On-line Image for Products, Brands, and the Corporation

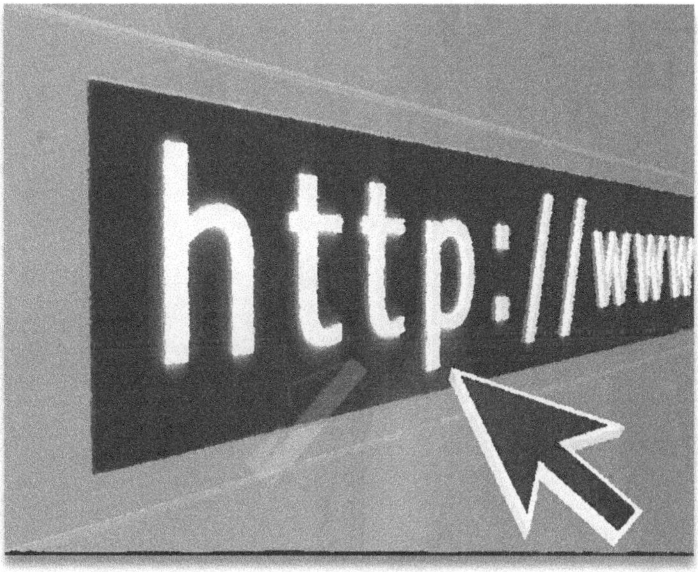

Image Management

When people are talking about your product, your brand, or your company then your finger needs to be right on the pulse and able to respond!

One key thing to remember that Googling this should bring your web-site to the top of the search, but what was said yesterday on a blog may take months to come to your attention even if you go through the first 100 pages of a Google search on a regular basis. Yet they can be highly visible in the social media world. The person that starts a hate campaign against your product or company needs to be

placated before the press come knocking on the door as a part of managing your image.

Image Management
• What is being said about
– my organisation?
– my brand/product?
– my competitors?
• Piracy? Legal?
• Developing a Social Media Intelligence
• Rewarding any recommendations
• Help people with problems

Image management is not limited to social media it is a traditional advertising and PR function that we are very familiar with. In the social media world it requires understanding of what is being said about your organisation, its brands and products. What is required is an ability to intelligently intervene for the good of the brand and its on-line image. This requires building a social media intelligence – a watching station, if you like, that keeps it eyes open at all times and enables people to respond appropriately.

Social media intelligence will enable you to know what is being said about your products at any time. Each business needs to have a plan that allows them to respond proportionately in any given situation. The triggers are criticisms etc. that need a response.

Is Social Media Just Another Broadcast Medium?

There are some that believe that Social Media is just another mechanism to broadcast a message to the masses. This belief has come about because the Internet has brought with it a 'democratisation' of broadcast media. Armed with a cheap video camera and an internet connection anyone can post whatever they wish to YouTube or Vimeo; but is that the image you wish to portray for your business?

It is true that for whatever we post there is an element of broadcasting. That new blog post is posted with the intent that everyone interested in our products or services will see it and will be swayed by our viewpoint. We also tell our social media connections in order that we are able to share the knowledge and in itself spread the news. Normally the intent here is to be seen as a thought leader, indeed we are in the process of using the Internet to build influence, improve reputation and engender trust. That element of broadcasting is about ensuring that our message gets out to all that have an interest in the subject.

When we use Social Media to tell our connections about the post then secretly we have a desire to make the message viral; to have the key influencers across the planet sit up and take note. Yet that is also coupled with anxiety of what will happen as a result of the viral message and whether the business can cope with the subsequent order uplift. In reality we know that our message will only be read by a small percentage of those in our network. It is with that small percentage that we are looking to move from a broadcast to a dialogue. Some of our connections will also be kind enough to pass it on to their network, which will add importance to our message.

This is the true impact of social media and our network. We bring all the power of LinkedIn, Facebook, Twitter, to bear in order to spread the word. Through the power of Social Media search the message can be seen by more than our direct network - it can be seen by those who have an immediate need, which can lead to new business connections and an uplift an sales. It is very much about building trust - place a good article, or video, and people will want to see more. When they see more and it all offers similar quality information they will start to trust you which will bring sales.

In addition to the things we post it is important that we are involved in the dialogue. This is the bigger picture. Jumping into the right conversation at the right time will also build trust. This however must add value and should never be taken as a platform to criticise our competitors product. Social Media is above all an ongoing conversation.

Remember that in society at large there is a level of mistrust, a cynicism that every message that put out is a con designed to separate the fool from his money. We mistrust government and party politics in general. It is through our posts that we seek to differentiate ourselves from these layers in society. We post to blogs in order to demonstrate our openness and willingness to interact with the marketplace at large and be involved in the key debates in the industry. In order to do this we must also be willing to admit our mistakes or errors. In the digital world it is almost impossible to hide anything. Instead we have to realise that the web is a great connector and our openness is an asset for doing business.

Intelligent Intervention

Another aspect of image management is an ability to intelligently intervene in the marketplace whenever things occur. The triggers here are questions about what is being said about any business, its products or the marketplace at large To some extent these can be viewed as traditional market research questions, but we have never before had such a powerful insight into people's thinking available every day on our desktops.

Social Media can go way beyond that level of thinking. It is possible to build an intelligence that is driven by what is important to people in the marketplace. It is also possible to link this general knowledge with a knowledge of the views of specific customers when they make any on-line contributions. This information is closely allied to marketing intelligence. Monitoring solutions are available that can automatically monitor internet buzz for you in order to identify what is important to customers and prospects.

This can also be used as a part of tracking possible piracy for music & film distributors. That person who loads a copy of their favourite track onto their website is breaching the law. How should the record company handle this? Is this a one-off occurrence or a big-time pirate.

The Twitter message "Smokey Robinson & The Miracles – "I Second That Emotion" ♫ http://blip.fm/~8..." may simply be a person pointing their friends as an on-line radio station and a favourite track that is currently playing – alternatively it may an indication of piracy in action. Whether action is taken is up-to the record company, but the point is that actions of others can be tracked.

Rewarding recommendations: What do you do when someone spontaneously say something good about your product and company? We should at the very least thank them, but the author has heard about an airline giving a 25% discount on flights because of something said on Twitter.

Helping people with their problems is one of the best ways of intervening. E.g. solving someone's PC problem will win a computer dealer kudos, even if the person does not use your product. What happens next time they are looking to buy a new computer? Of-course the proven expert will be very high on their list, if not the only candidate.

Developing Relationships

How we communicate with customers is changing. TV advertising, radio advertising, and perhaps newspaper and magazines adverts will continue to have a role to play as will advertising on the internet, but the ability to open a live dialogue with customers or prospect speaks volumes more than a pre-canned message pushed to a large audience.

Social media is more about the dialogue than it is a slick advertising message. Clearly with an advert there is space only for a short message, it has to fit into certain confines imposed on it. With having your own corporate website and associated blog it is possible to tell people about the power of the product, its capabilities, etc. The blog can also be include installation instructions, usage tips, and public announcements relating to new product development.

This allow us the opportunity to initiate a dialogue with anyone who is interested. It is also possible to do the same by solving other people's problems. This dialogue alone can convince the other person that you have something important to contribute. Building an ongoing dialogue should of-course focus on solving that person's problem, but it can open opportunities to connect and lay a foundation for trust based relationships to develop.

So should the connection be via a corporate persona, or through individuals employed by the company? Much will depend on the platform where the intervention takes place. A dialogue based on LinkedIn or Xing must be personal as those sites do not allow corporate personas. If the dialogue is based in Twitter, Facebook, or other sites it can be through the corporation as such a persona is allowed. Please do not break the rules defined by the site, this can result in your account being terminated, and your connections lost.

Developing Relationships

- No longer about *PUSH* communications
- Creating a dialog
- Personalised one-2-one communications
- Working with prospects
- Allowing people's voices to be heard
- Building real relationships with customers

Basically you are looking to build relationships through a series of communications channels. Always look to provide value through these communications, but also it is important to be cognisant to the needs of the other person. If it is clear the other person is a job-seeker, you should also see if there is a way that you can assist – even if there are no openings in your company then how you assist them now is likely to be repaid in business in the future.

Will Social Media Change how we use Advertisements?

Having analysed much of society it is this author's view is that advertisements will continue to be a part of the landscape on Web 1.0 and on Social Media sites well into the future. When used correctly advertisements can target the right market sector more precisely on social media channels than on any other communications medium. This may facilitate the movement of traffic to a target website more effectively that search engines alone.

The challenge is having the target person stop what they are doing for a few moments to pay attention, then take action by clicking the link to jump to your web site. Whether they stay will depend largely on presentation of your website and whether the product the company is selling really relates to the prospect's specific needs.

Leveraging Social Media also takes business beyond the act of advertising and as discussed earlier, the key components: Improving communications, collaborating more closely; Intelligently intervening in respect of things said about the product, brand, company, and marketplace; Each comes before the building of a revenue stream. It is essential to be seen as a market expert, and be seen as providing value, becoming a trusted resource. Leveraging Social Media is about more than marketing it is about connecting and communicating with your audience – engaging them even when they don't want something, but not doing so in a way that makes them feel you are chasing them for future sales. It is about being a resource to solve their problems. In fact Social Media can be a very effective customer service tool.

Erica Friedman, Social Media Optimizer and Publisher at ALC Publishing says "Advertisers are having major issues trying to understand the metrics associated with Social Media and are resistant to interacting directly with customers, except in very small, measured ways". These businesses seem to be measuring Social Media in the same way as they have measured any other media in the past. She also points out "Once upon a time, long before radio and TV, people had to talk to their customers, in order to keep their business going. The friendlier and more open and easy to work with, the better your business did. We're starting to see that model coming back, on a global scale". This is the important factor of social media that has is talked about in many parts of this book.

Social Media is about talking to the customer or prospect. Basically Social Media can simply be the platform by which a connection is made. It is still essential to win over the business, on human to human level, and that is about developing the relationship (whether through social media, the telephone, or face-to-face communications the choice ultimately depends on the customer).

Patrick Murphy of SiliconCloud makes the point that "that adverts are more targeted to your social media profile", well they have to be targeted to succeed on social media platforms. The 22 year old single woman sees a different advert than the 43 year old married man when they are on the same page at the same time. From the viewpoint of Facebook or LinkedIn this is the power of what they can offer an advertiser. Now whether the demographic focus of a specific product is right for the target audience is another question. That is where it is important to build a market intelligence for each product any corporation markets.

The reason it is important for corporations to leverage the power of Social Media as a part of there marketing communication strategy is as Firas Abo Assaf points out that according to a recent survey "80% of decision makers say they found the vendor, not the other way around" and "According to Marketing Sherpa, 80-90% of business to business transactions begin with a search on the web". With search engines becoming more Social Media aware the social media contributions made do become important. What this means is that buyers are increasingly aware of what they need and are researching the market before buying. This also has a relationship to the interaction with the marketplace through the Social Media channel. Buyers are looking for value from their suppliers and Social Media can be a part of that value chain.

The thought "Once upon a time, long before radio and TV, people had to talk to their customers" it seems society has come full circle, yet we are using different tools to facilitate this and the conversations are more public than ever before.

Further Reading and Related Articles:

A special thank you to the following LinkedIn members for their responses in this section:

Erica Friedman can be found at:

http://www.linkedin.com/in/ericafriedman

Patrick Murphy can be found at:

http://www.linkedin.com/in/murphyjpatrick

Firas Abo Assaf's information can be found at:

http://www.linkedin.com/in/firasassaf

Section 6

Turning our On-line Presence for Products, and Brands into Revenue

Revenue Opportunity

If you have read the pre-amble and opening chapters to get an understanding of Social Media then jumped straight to this chapter then you have missed some vital steps are urged to go back and read the last two chapters because without making improvements in the areas of communication and intelligent intervention on the web then you will not maximise your revenue opportunities through this new media.

Marketing has often been defined as communicating the benefits of your business's specific products or services to your prospects and customers. Yet it also needs to be so much more. Education of customer communities, understanding customer needs, and being involved in the dialogue are important parts of building a trust based relationship. Selling to people you are not in front of today is important and this is why this book have taken so much time looking at communications and image aspects. Social media is about building that trusting relationship and demonstrating expertise.

UK supermarket chain Tesco was one of the first to recognise that Business Intelligence combined with its reward cards could tell them so much more about the shopping habits of their customers, one of the reasons they have become the third largest retailer in the world. Yet this type of intelligence on its own cannot tell why individual shoppers did certain things. Take Joe Walsh, was diagnosed as having a rare allergy to oranges. Now Joe loved one particular fruit smoothie sold by his favourite supermarket, the reason he loved this particular product was that it gave him the all the tastes he had been craving for in a small bottle, which was on his shopping list every week. This fruit smoothie was unique in that it was based on apple juice rather than orange juice, which the majority of supermarket products were based on – a key differentiating factor for him.

One day Joe received from his supermarket a number of offers for free trials to juices that he knew were orange based, so naturally he binned these. About a month later his local supermarket ceased selling his favourite brand. When he enquired he was told the brand was no longer available. He was angered by this and called the company making the product who told him the product had been removed by the supermarket, but they still sold it in certain other stores, sadly none of those were in Joes area. The supermarket here clearly made a financial based decision rather than one based on specific customer knowledge.

This example was described without any social media intervention. The combination of reward cards and social media can allow a corporation to gain a clearer view of its customer's habits and their views. Clearly corporations must ultimately make financial decisions, but they can do so knowing a little more about the customer and their. Marketing communication has always succeeded based on how much trust the customer has in the company selling the product. The truth is that there are usually alternative selections available and if trust cannot be developed then the customer can always go elsewhere for their product, even if this means buying an inferior product.

Marketing communication is not simply about running an advertisement today and reaping the sales tomorrow. Even if that were true sometime in the past the world has become more complex today. Trust has become a key issue, even many loyal customers are questioning where they should make their next purchase. Social media is an important influence here. If you are not talking to your customer already on the medium then they may already be building trust in another supplier. We are all in business to make money and we must increasingly do this by solving our customers problems. This is as true for the public facing supermarket as it is for the corporation manufacturing industrial gas turbines.

Eight Statistics the Internet Marketer Should Consider

Retailer John Wanamaker is credited with saying "Half the money I spend on advertising is wasted; the trouble is I don't know which half". History has shown that the statistics are probably closer to 75% of advertising spend being wasted. Efforts have been made over the years to focus the advertising spend in the right areas, yet in reality Wanamaker's words are probably as true today as when he postulated them.

Marketing and the Internet has always been an interesting ground for statistics, so we thought this would be an ideal opportunity to look at a few:

25% of the worlds population currently use the internet a massive 1.7 billion people.

The number of users has grown by 380% in the last ten years. The biggest growth areas being the Middle East, Africa, and South America, but growth is occurring everywhere.

0.001% of all information stored on the internet has any relevance to my current goals.

Unable to credit any specific person with this quote and as time goes on the number of zeros between the decimal point and the 1 continues to grow.

On-line advertising response rates are typically lower than 2%.

This is well known and advertisers often forget there are two types of web user the person who is focused on a goal and the casual surfer. The focused person is not interested in the advert irrespective of its relevance – to respond is an interruption. The casual surfer only responds if an advert is relevant to them.

Visitors make a decision in just eight seconds whether to remain on a web-site.

Marketing Sherpa have given us this gem in their Landing Page Handbook. This writer knows from personal experience that there are some sites visited where the length of the stay is less than two seconds. So you had better make the page interesting.

Looking for information, services or products, more than 80% of Internet users rely on search engines.

Naturally without a direct link to the important information we have to search.

> *85% of these searchers don't click on sponsored or paid links.*

Interesting, maybe people are less inclined to support advertising feeling that un-sponsored links represent a fairer viewpoint. 63% of links appearing at the top of search results get the majority of clicks. This demonstrates the importance of good search engine optimisation.

> *59.8% of men and 67.2% of women go on-line while they're watching TV.*

We humans are multi-tasking creatures. Have laptop will multi-task. How much is this driven by television advertising is not known or are we all looking up the biographies of the stars of the latest hit show?

> *China has the largest number of Internet users at 384 million.*

Not bad for a country where democratic freedoms are limited. Yet plenty of sales opportunities do exist for the astute corporation.

Each of these has an impact if how we should be focusing many of our business development efforts.

A Trusted Advisor

How we buy things has changed. People are less influenced by slick advertisements; they are more impressed by what they know about the person they are buying from. Some of the challenges facing sales people is that they are discovering that the traditional buyer's priorities have changed. As a consequence sales in many sectors are either flat or declining significantly.

People and organisations have changed how they buy, what they buy, and how they evaluate vendors and partners. Because of the recent recession everyone is looking to save money. Yet this is only part of the problem. People have become conscious many of out past purchases have been wasted. E.g. the information system that cost the corporation millions of dollars is not being effectively used across the corporation. Today customers are looking for an effective solution to their problems. Corporations in particular are looking at how they can retain existing assets and leverage them to the fullest extent possible. Having a trusted third party that can bring in an objective view especially is focused on delivering specific solutions, and make savings at the same time.

This focus has changed over the last couple of years. Buyers are now looking to cost effectively solve problems. The impact can be that sales cycles becomes longer. Whilst this will not affect basic products like food it is impacting a lot of other aspects of our lives from consumer products to large business-to-business decisions.

The challenge in sales is in differentiation, and this is where social media can have a great impact – the buyer is more likely to listen to advice from their trusted network of connections than they are from a salesman, particularly if they leverage many of the traditional selling tactics. Competition is increasingly fierce. Your business must be able to demonstrate its message clearly to the marketplace and have the marketplace trust that message to be something that can be delivered. One key to becoming a trusted advisor is being actively involved in professional discussions in your marketplace through social media; to provide solutions; to offer value. Others relate to the whole sales approach taken that must be consistent.

The key change that has occurred in business at all levels is around the question of trust. That is why it has become more difficult to close sales. Decision makers listen to cold callers all of the time. There has become a change in how to manage sales this is linked to whether a trust-based relationship exists. Given that budgets are constrained and that corporations are under increasing financial scrutiny they no longer trust that the promised results and benefits will happen. Both trust and a visible Return on Investment (ROI) are vital components to winning any sale. There has become a lot of hesitation when making the decision to buy, particularly for big budget items.

The ability to close that gap, showing the buyer and decision maker that we can help them solve their problems is key.

The Psychology of the Buyer

Much of the reason why people or businesses are hesitant to make purchases is largely a matter of trust. It is not a lack of money or budget. The money is available people are just being prudent in their spending. The problem is not one of money it is largely a lack of trust. The sales cycle must therefore think about how that trust can be gained.

Traditionally sales has been characterised as being like a war. The trouble here is that it engenders conflict and one party wins while the other MUST lose. This does not engender trust. Certainly not if the salesman has foisted a worthless product on a buyer. These approaches simply do not work any more. Large segments of society believe that sales people are con-artists; saying or doing anything to make the sale. Therefore believability has become a real challenge. The reality is that selling, particularly cold-call based selling techniques are no longer trusted, no matter how genuine the person making the call.

Specific problem areas include:

- Applying pressure – getting the buyer to fold.
- Gimmicks, tricks – seen as artificial and fake
- Sales hype
- Adversarial role with customer
- Salesman has only their first interest at heart

The sales cycle now has to consider about how we are able to gain trust. This is one of the aspects where social media comes in. This media focuses on trust first and foremost. This is one of the reasons why this book spent such a large amount of time focusing in on:

- How we communication and collaborate; and
- The ability to intervene intelligently in the marketplace.

Being seen as contributing to market expertise as a vision leader and interested in solving other people's problems improves your trust quotient. That is how to unlock a real revenue stream through Social Media. Sales approaches need to be more consultative and more of a dialogue. Consider the following needs of the buyer:

- ✓ Someone who listens to their needs.
- ✓ To work with someone who is real, authentic and genuinely concerned about their problems – authenticity is important in judging the sales person.
- ✓ Seeks to build a partnership and work collaboratively.
- ✓ Is straight talking and honest.
- ✓ Client's best interest is the number 1 goal. E.g. providing real business value.

Involvement in social media, in particular being involved in the marketplace dialogue goes a long way to overcoming the psychological objections of the buyer.

Solving the customer's problems

Building trust is about what you say, what you do and how you do it. In essence though this is governed by the associated thought process. A choice has to be made to become a trusted advisor – become genuinely interested in solving the customer's problems.

It is important to be involved in a two-way dialogue with prospects and customers. You want to avoid giving any kind of sales pitch. It is important to focus on the customer's issues, needs, and challenges. So sales is not about what products can be offered, but problem solving. More specifically it focuses more on these challenges. Listening is a large part of this and understanding the other person's problem can go a long way to developing trust and rapport.

Revenue generation through social media is about the dialogue. It is important to be involved and have an understanding of your client's problems, this should always be based on an ongoing dialogue not on any assumptions about their challenges. We have talked about this being an ongoing dialogue, but it needs to involve a lot of conversations with many individuals. This is about the provision of real solutions to your customer's problems. The focus needs to be on the customer and their problem, not the products or services that you have for sale.

Again this is the reasoning behind the focus of this book, solving problems will lead to sales and build a longer term trusting relationship through the social media dialogue. There may be no immediate match, but because you have helped solve their problem there are likely to be future opportunities and you can turn this person into a genuine prospect.

Working with Human Nature

Humans are driven by the avoidance of anything that they perceive as uncomfortable, or painful, and are driven to anything that they perceive as providing pleasure or comfort. This explains why we love the latest and greatest "shiny new toy" it is also why young children will do anything to avoid eating broccoli when their parents tell them to eat their greens. The greatest mistake any business can make is to forget that humans make all the key decisions whether they are purchasing for themselves personally or for their business.

Some observations that can be made about human nature include:

- People believe that their problems are unique
- People want solutions to their problems
- People want assurance that they are making the right decision

This understanding drives how people think. With one breath in building a new business we talk about building a unique selling proposition (USP) yet there those who state that everything is predictable and there is no problem that has not previously been encountered.

Ever been into a suit shop and had the salesman take you by the hand and to the rack of suits they believe to be best suited to you? The problem here is they have no desire to understand your goals, they are simply trying to push product out of the door as fast as they can using their own pre-conceived notions about your needs. This is a part of a one-size-fits-all canned sales tactic that really needs to be consigned to the dustbin of history.

People today are seeking to have something exactly how they want it. We want to be treated as unique, and we expect those we do business with to understand and respond appropriately. In talking about becoming a trusted advisor it is important to listen to the needs of the customer – and these are specific to a particular moment in time, problems need to be solved quickly. Understanding the other person's problem is a vital aspect to winning business. Selling someone a navy-blue business suit when the need a grey wedding suit is a clear inability to listen and to get to the heart of the person's problem.

The USP is vital, it is what brings a business together with its customer. Every business must provide something that is unique and advantageous to the market. This distinguishes you from your competitor – uniqueness is of vital importance it is what gives you the edge over your competitor. In at least one aspect your competitor is always playing catch-up. How you solve customer problems can in itself become a unique advantage.

Being connected is vital, be it on the web through social media or in the physical world people respect those who are connected. It can be seen as being "one of us" which can be important for some customers. The demonstration of expertise and trust can go a long way to assuring the buyer that they are about to make the right decision. All this costs is the willingness to be involved in the community, a little time, yet the effort can often be repaid a hundred fold.

Connecting with others and building a powerful network is key to social media success. Leveraging that network will in itself bring new business.

Further Reading and Related Works:

John Wanamaker, a much respected and admired merchant, see the Wikipedia entry at:

http://en.wikipedia.org/wiki/John_Wanamaker

Internet World Statistics available at:

http://www.internetworldstats.com/stats.htm

Marketing Sherpa have given us this gem in their Landing Page Handbook, found at:

http://www.sherpastore.com/RevisedLandingPageHB.html

8 Steps To Becoming The Trusted Advisor – A Guide for Tech Sales by Ramon Vela, can be found at:

http://streetsmartsolutionprovider.com/sales-training-2/
8-steps-becomingthetrusted-advisor-guide-tech-sales/

Trust Agents by Chris Brogan and Julien Smith – ISBN-13: 978-0470-74803-9.

Section 7

The ROI of Marketing Through Social Media

The ROI of Social Media

Don't Set Aside the ROI in your Social Media Solution.

In looking at the use of Social Media within the workplace it is clear that what used to be almost universally banned as a diversion from real work is now becoming demanded as a tool to aid marketing communication and customer service.

It has become evident that social medial is no longer simply about chatting with friends and having fun. In fact people are now demonstrating their thoughts and feelings about a wide range of topics from Iran to the colour of their next handbag. Tastes, preferences and values are all being publicly displayed as users build a community and share their thoughts. If views are publicly available then they can be analysed. All this information this can be a boon for product planning and marketing communication.

Businesses are also getting involved in Social Media in order to:

- Build trust networks
- Collaborate with customers, vendors, and others
- Identify opportunities for growth.

Social Media can be viewed by many as the current must-have, but at what cost to the corporation? Are corporate executives setting aside the ROI in order to jump start their enterprise social media presence?

On the surface social media tools promise to connect the unconnected, but do they? In many corporations less than 100% of all workers have access to a PC, and many roles possibly will never include any factory worker access to computers, yet those workers still make a valuable contribution to the corporation. Social media through other devices such as mobile/cellular phones can increase accessibility and potentially add value. Because of the implementation of Instant Messaging (not strictly social media but it does demonstrates the benefits of on-line collaboration) in one corporation a warehouse supervisor spotted a potential error in a customer's delivery allocation that saved thousands in extra trucking costs – solved by Instant Messaging whilst the department manager was in a meeting and traditionally unavailable.

Contrary to Elizabeth Bennet's opinion in Feeling the Fear information sharing tools like wikis, video casts, and blogs can certainly contribute to a transformation of corporate behaviour. An ability to put information, instructions, training material into a wiki or a blog is of great importance. It takes on-line training one step further because the material was written by someone inside the organisation, and may even be someone the user knows. This is an additional factor not included in many ROI calculations.

It has been said that it is not possible to identify an ROI for collaboration improvements and that we only see the real improvements in the rear-view mirror. Yet looking back over years of many years of systems implementation it is possible to define an ROI for any proposed solution. This is about producing a best estimate available at the time the need is perceived. That is as relevant for any Social Media implementation as it is for any other corporate change. Remember here the major impact of social medial is more in the area of business than with the technology that underpins it. Implementation does not require a technology project, but it does require planning.

Internally setting up of blogs and wikis has business challenges in respect of convincing people of the need to make contributions. People are often keen to initially get involved, but keeping contributions coming after the initial setup is even more vital. This is where the real work occurs in the building of any corporate knowledgebase. Sharing needs to be encouraged through the organisation. This requires a change in mindset, yet many people are already willing and have skills to do it because of their ability to contribute to discussions on Facebook, Twitter, LinkedIn, and other social networks.

There is no intention to enter the realm of the impact on the corporate psychology of collaboration, that is important but outside the scope of this book. The whole area of social media is always questioned as to whether contribution in the area of social computing (e.g. blogs, wikis, social networks) whether internal or external constitute real work. This argument must form part of the ROI for Social Media.

Social Media meets BI:

Finding Social Media's Business Value

With the rise of every new business tool comes the need to leverage it correctly in order to provide real business value. This book discussed earlier the preparedness to intervene when people are talking about your brand and having a plan to responding appropriately. Social Media intelligence is about managing that intervention.

Business Intelligence is traditionally capable of measuring business performance via a number of indicators. Traditionally the majority of these are financial indicators relate to the corporate balance sheet and are an indication of corporate performance. However many global corporations measure activities that have no immediate link to the balance sheet, such as production cycles. In the same way it is possible to measure the contribution made by Social Media to the business.

There are however several aspects that we do need to consider in looking at the value proposition made by Social Media to the business:

- The value of enhanced communications and collaboration.
- The ability to listen and understand what is being said about us.
- Responding appropriately to customers/prospects.
- Engaging the marketplace.

There is value to be gained from improving collaboration within the workplace. We have to consider that for every employee there is a sphere of influence radiating out from themselves through their team into the company at large an even influencing those outside the organisation. This collaborative sphere should be seen as one that adds value. However through the use of Social Media the company is investing in relationships. We must remember that collaboration is much more than communications it is about the right people being involved when appropriate. These experts can be found across the business in all roles, it may be as little as the truck driver who knows that customer delivery schedules, or it may be the analyst assesses the viability of routes who discovers that the delivery schedule can be rationalised and made more efficient. The whole organisation is working together for common benefit.

Listening and understanding what is being said about any business is an important factor for success. For example the music industry has always employed talent spotters on the street who are listening out to the youth to see who the latest upcoming artists are, yet this reach can only go so far. Social Media adds an extra dimension to this capability. Being in-tune with what is being discussed can allow a prospective talent to be identified without a talent scout being in the locality.

Listening and understanding applies to all types of businesses, but how? Googling your brand or company should show your web-site to the top of the search results, but it is unlikely to show what someone just said about you on Twitter. Using traditional search engines (like Google and

Bing) takes time and a lot of effort to discover what was said yesterday, let alone an hour ago. The social media landscape is busy and plenty of noise so monitoring searches on Twitter can also waste time, a resource that is precious in any business. The challenge is to identify and hear the conversations happening on blogs, social networks, forums, news sites, and more. You will need tools that allows you listen to millions of conversations in real-time without having to waste time. It is important to respond appropriately. Remember a majority of the time a simple thank you frequently goes a long way.

It should be noted that Social Media is a two way street. Part of listening is being seen to be paying attention. If someone follows you then you should consider following them back. CNN has over 150,000 followers on Twitter yet the service only follows a handful of people. Following back is an essential part of being responsive. That is not to say you follow everyone blindly, again business guidelines are required here, but you should consider following competitors, customers, prospects and market experts at a minimum.

Responding appropriately is a vital component. Giving away a free flight because a passenger praised your airline's check-in procedure may not be a proportionate response. The strategy should be decided upon within the marketing department, yet be executed across the company.

Engaging the marketplace is perhaps the most important aspect that can win new business. In researching this book the author identified how a Customer Services representative at Dell Computer answered a question on Twitter about a

Windows problem, because Dell customer service answered the question they gained a friend in the overall PC user community. The expertise is not about answering questions on your product, or brand, but giving fair advice even on your competitor's products, and also responding to general discussions in the marketplace.

Remember also that monitoring competitor information in Social Media is as simple as investigating your own performance. Here everything is open an visible to all. Social Media is full of opinions and counter-opinions, these change almost by the hour and can be influenced by a wealth of factors. If you are not monitoring your competitors they will be monitoring and measuring you.

Engaging the marketplace is about being seen as the expert, the 'person' everyone wants to listen too. This is about building trust, being the market expert. It is also quite possible to be considered an expert by a person that you only know on-line, this is a part of the new psyche of doing business. This is where trust adds value.

Business Intelligence is though about the ability to measure the value in the things that we do for the business. Normally BI measures $ value, $ costs. Social Media Intelligence is more a process of discovery of the things being talked about. Yet measurement is still important. It should be a valid business goal in real-time to track and measure campaigns, brands, products and sentiment (positive, negative or neutral), and provide additional context by analysing results over time, as well as comparisons with competitors.

The Interplay of Social Media, Business Intelligence, and Cost Effectiveness

Social Media, Business Intelligence, and Cost Effectiveness are three major business issues that are rarely put together in the same sentence. Yet all do have a role to play in improving business results.

From the ability to leverage Social Media as a media and Customer Services tool that allows a business to communicate more effectively. The advantage of good business intelligence is in the ability to leverage the in broad based information set that we have about historical and present company performance, adding in future forecasts and an analytical capability to improve the decision making process. It does not stop there. Better decisions plus increasing efficiencies and the unique selling proposition give the business a competitive advantage. These are key business drivers.

On the cost effectiveness front most corporations have severely limited budgets, having to do more with less money so building new systems is for many simply out of the question. This is one area where most Social Media solutions bring good news, for most there is no massive systems deployment. In fact it is possible to leverage Social Media solutions with a zero systems outlay – that figure looks good on the spend side of any business. Yet there is a cost in leveraging Social Media, but it comes in other ways:

◊ Social Media advertising

◊ Person-Time with corporate on-line intervention

Push advertising differs little on Social Media other than an improved ability to speak directly with your target audience. If you are selling shoes and your primary market is 16 to 30 year old women then Social Media advertising can focus on that group. Most of the existing sites can very effectively break down their membership and allow you access to your target audience. You will not get an email address, simply access to their on-line presence, provided they a part of your target demographic.

On-line advertising has always been accompanied by a low click-rate. Social Media improves this because your message can be specifically focused for different groups, but you do have to remember that the message must fulfil their exact needs right now. E.g. "I have been looking for one of those..." otherwise people won't even look at your advert. People have learned to tune-out on-line adverts at an early stage in their on-line life because most of the messages were not for them. The mentality still exists, but not people do spend a large amount of time in front of their trusted Social Media sites and messages can be present for longer than the 30 second TV commercial.

One of the aspects business intelligence brings to this situation is the ability to measure the impact of social media efforts to your corporate website. Visits to the corporate site can have a different entry point for social media than for a Google search. The actions can be measured, where they have been, what they have done, how long they stayed, etc.. Ultimately that intelligence can be fed-back into the knowledge cycle and allow the corporation to further refine its intervention.

Being seen to be paying attention is a key aspect. In Social Media a listening corporation is one who responds to what is being said, even if this means taking one on the chin – admitting faults when they exist. Of-course remember that some people have an axe to grind and few efforts will placate them. but at the end of the day it is important to be seen to respond in a reasonable manner. More so than ever before everything that is said is available to 6 billion people across the planet – some right now may care little about your product but people tend to have a long memory for problems. In this respect it may be better to admit the fault and update everyone on the progress of the replacement than go into a traditional denial mode.

The point here is that without a social media strategy your corporation will not know how to respond but with one the response can be timely, direct, and proportionate.

Further Reading and Related Works:

Elizabeth Bennet's opinion in Feeling the Fear from CIO Insight June 2009 is found at:

http://www.cioinsight.com/c/a/Trends/Feeling-the-Fear-but-Doing-It-Anyway-324289/

Section 8

Bonus Articles – Leveraging Social Media throughout the Corporation

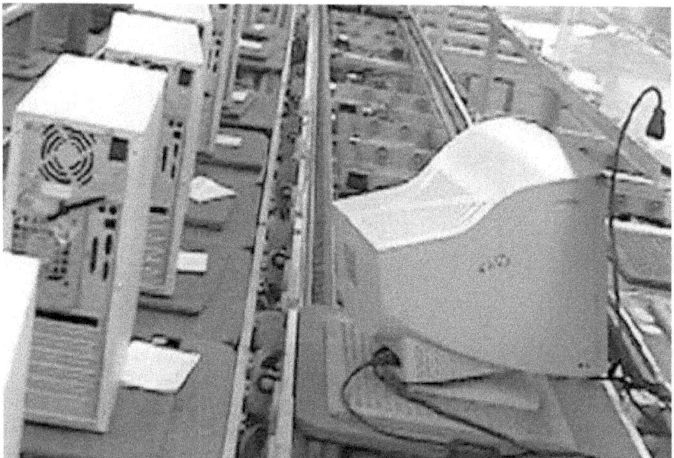

For the Hiring Manager

Hiring through Social Media

Much has been written about meeting the challenges of sales and marketing through the use of social media, yet there are many other uses for the service. CRM has been discussed. Hiring is certainly another area where social network connections can make a difference. LinkedIn, Facebook, Twitter, Namyz, Zoominfo, and other sites can all assist in the job search, but that is not their primary reason to exist. Job seekers are actively leveraging their on-line network in search of their next role. For every job seeker there is also a hiring manager wishing to fill a role.

Hiring managers also need to understand how they can leverage the social media solutions they already use to connect with potential new staff members. Do not think purely of using these sites as a means of advertising a role when it does become available. Think of ways to connect with prospective employees with every thing that you do online, not simply at the time you need a specific hire.

When It comes to bring ready to make a new hire firstly you should look through your own connections before taking any other steps. You may already be in touch with the ideal candidate. The other alternative is that someone you know will be connected to the ideal candidate and may be able to connect you. The next article discusses a number of methods to leverage what LinkedIn has to offer in order to identify potential candidates. As each social medial site differs in its approach, but they all offer tools that allow you to connect with other people and that is key here. The recruitment consultants and advertising should almost be the place of last resort, not the first place you focus on.

When you have looked at your own network and are unable to identify any candidates then It is time to find other ways to connect with them. For example all LinkedIn groups have 'jobs' sections where posting jobs is easy and it is easy to post a link to the job posting through Twitter or Facebook. The key aspect about this media is that It demands interaction. That is as true for the hiring manager as it is for the person seeking new employment. If you have seen a clear insightful comment on the media and thought you would like to hire that person at an opportune time, well now that you have such a need they should be your first call, even if you know them to be employed and happy in their job.

Don't be afraid to ask the people you know to see if they can make recommendations, that is after all about leveraging your network. We know this is the best way to make an effective hire, which also saves the business money in the recruitment process. The key is participation, attention, and sometimes a little patience. Most hiring managers know the talent they require many months in advance of the formal recruitment process starting, use this time wisely to make connections that can help you get in touch with perspective candidates.

At the end of the day there are plenty of options available to use before turning to a recruitment agent, who have proven to be less than reliable in recent times.

Finding Staff through LinkedIn

With the range of social media tools available combined with the wealth of information that active members do provide on-line it is surprising that more hiring managers do not turn to social media channels for all of their recruiting needs.

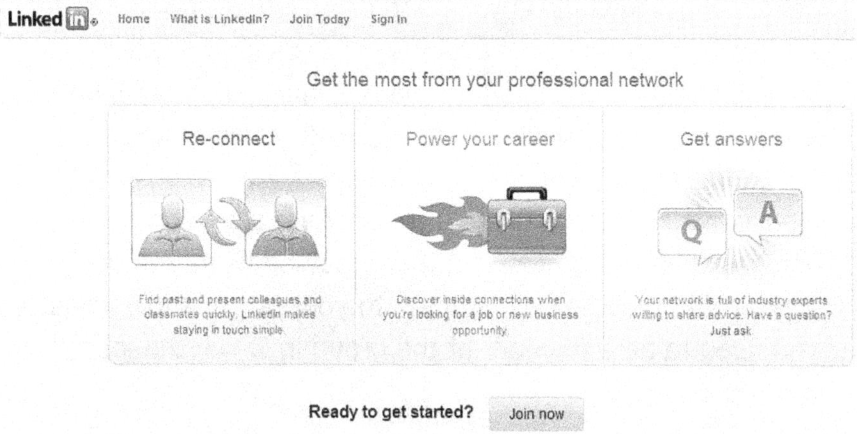

LinkedIn's sign-up page talks about powering your career, specifically "discover inside connections when you're looking for a job or new business opportunity". The site's power comes from an ability to connect people sharing common goals. It is about building a professional network on-line and leveraging for many aspects of business. Looking specifically at LinkedIn there are several job boards on the site ranging from the main job site where posts are paid for to the groups where members of the group can post a job at no cost.

Jobs: vp
edit | X
V. P. Government Relations at Toronto 2015 Pan American Games Host Corporation
VP/Director, Inside Sales at FreshBooks
Vice President, Corporate at MS&L Worldwide
See more »

Paid postings will be viewable by anyone performing a job search with matching criteria and can even be configured to appear in a column on the user's main page. Potentially viewable by any of the 50 million plus members. Costs here are comparable to posting on specialist job sites like JobServe.com or Monster.com. Groups are arguably a better alternative in that posts are free, they are also more focused. The problem is that there may be twenty or thirty groups that may be relevant and to your target audience and you need to be a member of the group in which the job posting is placed.

Posts on the group also rely on the member having the right notification settings in-place, but the active job hunter is more likely to be paying attention to these openings than others, the advantage of group job posts is that they are free. One potential disadvantage is that the poster has to be a member of the group. It is recognised that many hiring managers have different interests to their employees and therefore other than for hiring will not be interested in group activity. There is nothing stopping the manager joining that group temporarily then leaving once they have a set of likely candidates.

LinkedIn is a very powerful site for professional networking. As such It does not matter whether you are a hiring manager, a job-seeker, or simply using it to make business connections, LinkedIn should be used in a similar fashion. You should always seek to make professional connections

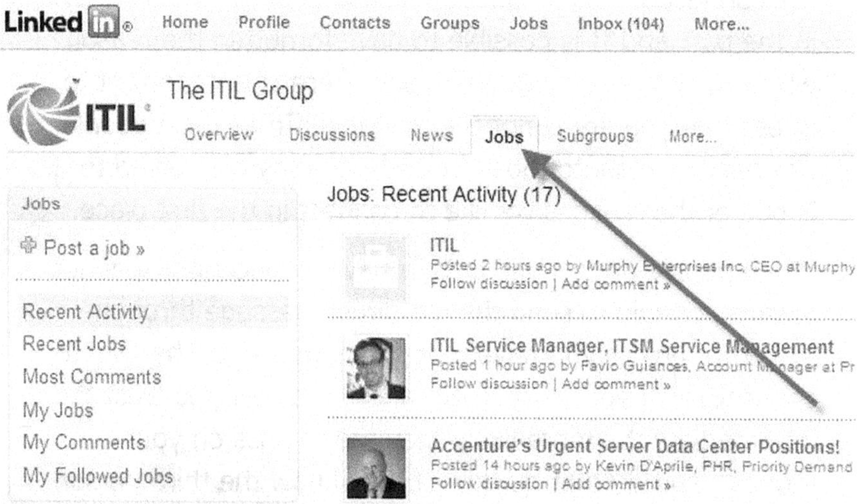

that can assist your goals.

The first challenge is always finding a potential candidate. For this LinkedIn has very good search capabilities. It should be possible to find a large pool of people with the right background. It is best advised to start with broader criteria than narrow requirements. For example use the term 'CRM' rather than the name of a specific software package when looking for a CRM Analyst. Once you have a pool of potential candidates then take a look at their profiles. You may be surprised at the number of first level connections you have that already fit your criteria. These are the easiest to contact because you already have access to their full email contact details through your personal connections, and generally speaking it is best to make the approach via email rather than LinkedIn's internal message system as sadly many users do not always pay attention to their LinkedIn internal notifications.

If you know the person remind them where from. Many of the connections come about because of social media activity in the past and It is possible to have forgotten the reason why you connected two years ago. Here It is important to stress that you are connected on LinkedIn as most people are willing to talk to those they are already connected to; it is one of the reasons we like to connect in the first place.

When people are second or third level connections it is not always possible to send them a direct message through LinkedIn, unless you have a premium account. The way to connect is via another person, and the better you trust the intermediary the more likely they are to pass on your request, and do that quickly. If they know the third person well they may be prepared to facilitate an introduction face-to-face or via email. Beware that you may be connected to the prospective employee only via their existing manager, who is a part of your network – not the best connection point to the perspective employee.

LinkedIn can also be used in many ways to identify potential candidates. Once specific people have been identified It is important to find out more about them and gain further insights about their suitability for the role in question. Their activity on LinkedIn Answers, and their activity in the groups they belong to may speak volumes about them.

LinkedIn Answers is a great way of connecting with some potential candidates. One suggestion is to pose a question that is linked to a real life scenario the successful applicant would face in their job. Look at each of the replies and communicate with people as they respond to your question. It is true that not all answers you receive will be relevant, but those that are provide an opportunity for opening up a dialogue – tell them that you are currently seeking to hire someone into a role where this scenario represents one of the key challenges. They may be able to recommend someone for the role, or be interested themselves. It is important not to think about where people are located as often people on the other side of the planet have connections that are local to you or they may be an expatriate wishing to return home.

In conclusion this may indicate that there is work for a hiring manager to complete in order to find good quality candidates, but through LinkedIn it is possible to identify people without spending anything but time; and ultimately that will please the accountant.

Is it a job that can be handed off to HR? As a hiring manager I have always advocated that HR have no involvement in the recruitment process; they simply do not possess the skills necessary to decide whether any individual has the right technical knowledge for the job; and certainly should not be allowed to pre-screen candidates. They may need to be involved at some stage during the recruitment process, but can have problems with unconventional routes to finding candidates. If you do hand off this process to anyone then you should involve a person the new recruit would work closely with once they are employed rather than HR.

Social CRM: Uncovering a Customer Insight

For many years it has been an important business goal to uncover insights within customer behavioural dynamics. This requires the business to focus their marketing communication efforts through a customer intelligence solution.

Normally this is achieved by combining the use of advanced analytics with analytical CRM components. This is one form of closed-loop Business Intelligence, the principle of which is to predict behaviour based on classes of customer. Of course a class can be encompass a group of one person, but is normally much larger. The concept is that each customer would fall into certain demographic groups. There are certain behaviour patterns that could be drawn from the generalised behaviour of specific groups of people. We are now living in different times and whilst group behaviour can still assist in determining the general needs of a group it does not assist in knowing why individual customers make specific choices.

Take Joe, he is 52 years old, middle class, owns a Mercedes on many things he is typical for his age group, a true red-blooded American, supports his college football team. On the management team where he works. He is involved with many local causes. A family man with three kids, staunchly conservative on most issues, yet a vegetarian since his youth. His whole family have followed him in this regard with each making a conscious choice.

When the local supermarket sends them special offers it is always for meat products that nobody in the family eats. This is a case of the store fitting him and his family into specific demographic groups and having little tolerance for individual preference within their data structures. For most things Joe and his family follow the norms associated with their demographics. Through traditional Business Intelligence it is possible to identify specific anomalies to demographic norms, yet there is a tendency to believe that Joe's family purchase their meat from another store; hence the offers that are sent.

UK supermarket chain Tesco has performed much research in making special offers relevant to their customers, yet it is all too easy to make assumptions. Thus it is all too easy to misunderstand why people do the things they do. We may never truly understand why people do all they do, even with a psychologist on the business team.

What social media adds to the picture can be the views and attitudes of the customer. However to add value these must drive additional insight over and above the demographic norms. For small businesses there is often more value driven by listening to customers than can be gleamed from analytics. Of course small businesses have to think twice before adding expensive systems.

Social CRM: Business Intervention Requires Extra Capabilities!

Customer Relationship Management solutions have sadly been misunderstood by many. Normally they are defined as the system for managing customer data, but in reality it should be so much more; the core process by which the corporation manages all its interactions with customers and prospects. When you add social media into the corporate domain then how we manage customer relationships changes, hence the term Social CRM. Businesses are no longer simply managing that relationship through telephone, or face-to-face meetings. The customer may be communicating through a mass of other channels and every business needs to be listening.

Twitter, Facebook, and other social channels can tell us so much about the customer's intentions, motivation, and thinking. This needs to be integrated with other insights about the customer. The CRM solution needs to actively integrate customer social profiles to make this happen.

Currently the majority of CRM solutions are not social media aware, let alone able to manage an active integration of all the components. This change will occur, but sadly to date the majority of installed solutions are limited in their capability. Can your existing solution handle the following:

- extended customer profiles
- customer insights
- collaborative insights

- enterprise collaboration

Extended customer profiling must include links to the many social sites the customer and their key decision makers are active on. These links need to be active links in order to allow specific CRM users access to customer thinking. This can impact the whole way that relationship is managed.

The term 'active link' in this context will allow the CRM user to jump directly from the customer profile to a specific social site, and even recognises the possibility that a customer may have many profiles being active on many sites. All CRM solutions include notes fields, these are not appropriate for long term storage of social links.

Drawing out customer insights is a vital aspect of social media intervention. There is only limited value of being active without measuring the customer's insights. The term 'measuring' was used deliberately in this context. For larger corporations these customer insights need to be measurable, through the Business Intelligence solutions and add value to customer interactions. It can allow us to be more responsive. We can also become more proactive in managing that relationship.

Collaborative insights can involve a wide range of people, including industry experts. This allows the business to manage its intervention in the marketplace more effectively, being more responsive to changing market conditions. Ever thought of involving your customers in your product development efforts? Everyone has an opinion and on many of the social media channels people are not afraid to give them. For the listening corporation there are many new ideas available, including the insights that can be gleamed from within the enterprise. These can cover a range of ideas and certainly go beyond the old fashioned suggestion box.

One thing is certain social media is not simply another advertising channel. Business intervention is required to make the most of the channels. The CRM is a business tool that can aid in that intervention.

Breaking out of the Rut of Poor Service Standards

Despite all of the technological advances we have made in the area of customer relationship management (CRM) it seems that the companies having an active technological solution are some of the leaders in complaining about their own poor customer satisfaction ratings. Even companies that believe they provide excellent customer service find their customers disagree.

We are all familiar with the story of callers getting trapped inside the interactive voice response (IVR) systems. Emails go unanswered, and there is no local presence - the nearest office being two thousand miles away. Then when the customer finally does get through it is to an agent does not possess the correct skills to resolve their problem.

Therefore business seems to be somewhat at an impasse as far as its customer interface is concerned. Is the problem solved by more or better technology? No. All too many organisations talk about developing a caring attitude to their customers, yet fall short on execution. Keeping a customer satisfied is a daunting task and it lies beyond any statistics that can be produced. People want to be treated like people, with some respect. The problem may not be important in the eyes of the customer services agent, but it can be vital to the customer. Getting through to a person is important and customers do not appreciate waiting for forty minutes at a time in order to find an agent who is unable to assist. Ultimately this leads to the belief that this corporation does not care about its customers.

Some problems begin by over-hyping the capabilities or create unrealistic customer expectations, leading to frustrated buyers, when they open the box. Does technology offer any assistance here? Yes it can. Getting that easy to assemble flat-packed furniture home and laying it out on the carpet the customer cannot even see whether all the parts are present, let alone start the assembly process. Video instruction manuals on the corporate blog, that are easy to find with the web address marked clearly on the packaging is a start (indeed some corporations used to provide an instruction video for such products).

Automation assists most corporations is ensuring that many processes are made more efficient and can assist the savvy customer e.g. automated hotel checkouts. But these tend to only assist in the simplest of situations and all too frequently the frustrated guest joins the lengthy check-out queue, because the automated solution could not resolve the problem. Again no person to assist here.

Getting smarter is not necessarily about extending automation, it may not be about replacing the CRM system, it is more about how business thinks about its customer interactions. The customer service element of running our business has been treated as a business expense where costs can be cut or ultimately eliminated. Some web-based businesses believe in the zero customer service model. In reality this should not considered as a part of any business model.

Having customer service in mind does mean having the right level of technological and people support available. It also means refocusing our efforts around the customer and their preferred support channel. Defining the right customer service budget plays a key part of costing any new product or service. Having knowledgeable people available is always key.

Productivity and Social Networks

There has long been a fear that the introduction of social networks will impact the level of productivity within the workplace. Of course the word that most people add into that sentence is "negatively". The assumption being that the workforce will be spending their time on Facebook, or Twitter, instead of working. Twittering their time away, if you can excuse the pun.

Yet there is so much more to social networking than people simply busying themselves with non-work activities, indeed even without the addition of social networks there were dozens of ways to avoid work, indeed new ones will be invented by those that wish to avoid work. Work avoidance may be a skill as old as the concept of work itself.

The fact is that social networks can, if used correctly, bring many benefits to an organisation. If we think of the programmer who is facing a technical problem, they will discuss this problem with others in his team, should the solution not be evident they will seek advice from others that they know, they will use their network. Part of this advice may come from on-line communities, indeed every programmer knows which network to be involved in to get the answers, or even to contribute themselves. Indeed contribution is important as people tend to help those that help others.

Yet it is always right to question who in any organisation will benefit from being involved in Social Networks. One of the impacts of the popularity of social media is the fact that there are many purveyors of material that can lead viewers to dangerous sites. There is a public misconception that we are safe on-line, yet it can be the source of phishing attacks and other malware. This is where the corporate security solution needs to be capable of stopping such intrusions. Yet some of this intrusion can be managed by educating the workforce about on-line behaviour.

The same is true of legal risk and treats to reputation, both corporate and personal. Writing complaints about work frustrations or giving away work secrets is also a matter of having a corporate policy of what is or is not acceptable behaviour. The key aspect here is that not everything that is said in a work environment is repeatable on your Facebook status, in fact the majority of things discussed in the work environment should never be repeated to the outside world. In this regard employment contracts will need to change in order to place a duty on every employee to keep this material confidential. That hot insider news is not for public consumption, even if you have the tool at hand to achieve instant world-wide publication. Much information is so secret that it is not even for internal consumption within that organisation.

Anyone involved in product or corporate development will have confidentiality clauses in their employment contracts - a breach of which can lead to termination of employment.

How employees are involved with social networks will be impacted by how they are trained. Sending that embarrassing photograph home via email and publishing it in personal time on Facebook is as damaging as doing it during work time. Yet if a CEO, or another corporate officer, is found to be behaving inappropriately then arguable this should be published for all the world to see.

There is more benefit to be attained through the social networking interactions than simply blocking all these sites. Is it appropriate for an order processing clerk to be using Facebook at work? Perhaps not, but is may be appropriate for someone in Marketing or Customer Services to be doing so as a part of managing a brand reputation.

Trends

Seeing predictions by analyst firm Gartner it is always important to sit up and take notice. The predictions do however need to be translated into strategic business thinking. This is especially true for social and collaborative software right now. Predicting the future is always a complex thing and much depends on focus and perspective.

Mark R. Gilbert, VP Research at Gartner states "success in social software and collaboration will be characterised by a converted and collaborative effort between IT and the business." Actually all software implementations should be a part of a collaboration between the business community and IT as its change agent. Is this true for social media deployment?

For many small and medium sized corporations there can be a very minimal start-up costs to deploy a social media solution. It is simply a matter of leveraging existing employee's free time and being involved in the available social media channels. For larger corporations this demands management and co-ordination, but can often be managed without adding any personnel. The majority of the costs involved will normally be associated with building a social media intelligence capability. This intelligence capability is crucial for monitoring things said in the media about the company's product or brand, and ultimately the marketplace in which the corporation functions. Response needs to be immediate and proportionate, yet demonstrate expertise and build trust. If the answer is "that is not possible" then tell people why.

Gartner's analysts predict that only 25 percent will routinely use social network analytics to improve performance. Sadly corporations have not benefited as they should have from analytics in the past. Today however successful use of social media depends on it. Furthermore the analytical capability needs to be tied directly to customers or prospects. Without this there can be significant wasted or misdirected effort.

"By 2014 social networking services will replace email as the primary vehicle for interpersonal communications for 20% of business users". Email is likely to remain for the immediate future as the primary means of confidential communications. If not email then products like Google Wave will allow confidentiality and collaboration within a single product. There are many other ways to communicate in short, sharp bursts, such as IM, that are batter than email, even today. Many in the business community associate these products with home use; a way to connect with their daughter after she has gone off to college; they have so many more uses than social chit-chat. Business will simply become more confident with their value over the next few years. Changing modes of work does mean that more people are telecommuting and social networking solutions are already expanding this.

Gartner talks about organisations looking for a corporate 'Twitter', yet such options do exist right now, take a look at Yammer. There are limitations to corporate only sites of this nature, one being an ability to connect with external experts (for Yammer the email address must belong to the corporation concerned, the scale of Twitter is one of the key reasons for its success.

Who should lead the social media adoption initiative? From the perspective of this writer such initiatives should be led by a clear business imperative with IT becoming the agent of change. The business must have a desire to drive the project forward on a corporate level in order for success. Departmental initiatives can only meet with limited success.

One aspect about social media is that it still needs to be fully supported by a unified communications strata, a common approach for PCs, smart phones, and other devices. This will improve the collaborative opportunities across business communities. The younger generation will be pushing for this capability. Some exploration has been made in this area, but there is no single unified active social media dashboard available today. As Gartner correctly state for some users these social applications will be the first and only applications they use.

It is essential to develop a corporate strategy, policies and governance around social media. This particularly impacts how customer interactions are managed. Trust is key to the future and this is as applicable In the B2B world as it is in consumer facing businesses.

Defining Social Media policy

In defining any type of corporate policy it is important to understand the type of organisation that the policy is set for. Any two bodies, even those competing in the same marketplace will have different professional standards and ethical limits. This will impact how policies are defined for any discipline in that business.

In respect of social media implementation then each corporation will have different goals. Some will see leveraging social networks to drive value from customer engagement as of vital importance while others do not.

As discussed before certain information should never be made public. For example, it would be a serious breach of medical ethics for a doctor to discuss specific patient details on any on-line forum. Yet ironically they should be encouraged to publish professional material on blogs, e.g. papers, or discussion articles, that would normally be published in a medical journal, this contributes to improving their own professional standing.

Employee use of social networks should be consistent with acceptable use policies for the Internet as a whole, yet much will depend on the employee's role within the organisation. The customer service agent now needs to be able to connect with customers on the sites they congregate at.

The availability of easy publication mechanisms has led to some employees taking a rather *laissez-faire* attitude to the confidentiality of the information they have access to. Pre-existing employee guidelines normally prohibit distribution of this information. However corporate management should re-examine their policies and ensure all employees are aware of their duties.

Education is another important aspect here. All too often policies are presented to new staff upon arrival in their new job, then never referred to again except in cases of serious breach. Education acts as a reinforcement to that policy and should be mandatory during the course of employment.

Protecting company secrets has always been high on the priority list for business. Just because it is now easy to publish something on the web does not mean we should. Confidence is always a key factor in any business. Risks to be considered include personal data, customer data, and business reputation.

P3 Social Media

Connecting the Unconnected

Call us:

905 371 3908 (Toronto)

646 875 4558 (New York)

http://p3socialmedia.com/

Connect with Peter B. Giblett at:

http://linkedin.com/in/pgiblett

http://twitter.com/pgiblett

http://facebook.com/pgiblett

Dust Jacket Information:

Do you know what Social Media is? You should do! if you are currently looking at promoting your business through the Internet then you need to take a long hard look at Social Media. This new media is connecting people as we have never been connected before. It enhances your corporation's web media strategy, introducing a new dimension, that relies on human interaction.

This media is not simply for staying in touch with friends, it also affords any business the opportunity to be in touch with customers, prospects, and others who share a general interest in the particular marketplace. An ability to communicate has always been key to selling, yet the customer is interested in becoming more involved in the products they use, possibly to the extent of influencing their development.

Social Media more than anything facilitates communications between interested parties, which in turn allows businesses to be able to build powerful customer relationships based on trust. Through the media you can build a loyal customer following, expand your brand and generate a buzz, often led by the customer.

Peter Giblett is a leading social media strategist and has helped corporations identify the correct way to leverage this new media. He explains what social media is and how best to use it. He provides real-life examples and best practices in leveraging social media to drive business success.

Success is about being connected to customers, prospects, staff, industry experts, and even competitors. Reputation is important, and through corporate social media presence a level of trust can be built. If you want to learn how to build your business through Social Media then "*Is your Business Ready? For the Social Media Revolution*" will show you how.

www.ingramcontent.com/pod-product-compliance
Lightning Source LLC
Chambersburg PA
CBHW071148050326
40689CB00011B/2021
* 9 7 8 1 4 5 2 8 4 6 8 0 4 *